ADVANCE PRAISE

"This book is the book that I wish I had when I started my journey as an educator. More urgently, it's the book that I wish my teachers had a generation ago. As we face a future anchored in the cold individualism of our now, Venet's work is not just important, it has the ability to recast our collective future into something more healthy, more human—more powerful."

—Cornelius Minor, educator and author of *We Got This: Equity, Access, and the Quest to Be Who Our Students Need Us to Be*, Brooklyn, New York

"This is the book on trauma-informed education I've been waiting for. Practical and inspirational, affirming and challenging, patient and urgent, Venet invites us to consider the political dimensions of trauma and healing, correctly steering us away from savior narratives of damage and rescue and instead toward dreams of collective well-being and justice."

—Carla Shalaby, author of *Troublemakers: Lessons in Freedom from Young Children at School*

"*Equity-Centered Trauma-Informed Education* is brimming with timely and critical insights. Classroom teachers and school leaders will find it expansive in scope, intimate and engaging in style, and actionable in content. Crucially, Venet centers antiracism and social justice as fundamental to trauma-informed schooling, making this a vital resource for educators."

—Elizabeth Dutro, Ph.D., Professor, School of Education, University of Colorado Boulder, author of *The Vulnerable Heart of Literacy: Centering Trauma as Powerful Pedagogy* (Teachers College Press)

"*Equity-Centered Trauma-Informed Education* should be required reading for every educator and education leader. Alex Shevrin Venet has written an accessible, practical book that offers proactive strategies for supporting children's healthy development and the learning process. She effectively focuses on shifts in how to think about and approach education in our classrooms and schools. An important addition to the field."

—Cindy Johanson, Executive Director, Edutopia

"Alex Shevrin Venet's book has provided a critical framework for trauma -informed practice that centers the goals of educational equity and liberatory education. Teachers, administrators, district, and state leadership would be well served by applying this perspective as they aim to serve their students and communities. These are the principles and perspective shifts we need to radically transform our nation's future mental well-being for the better."

—Colleen Wilkinson, Director of Montessori Country Day School Houston and Consultant at Trauma Informed Montessori

Equity-Centered Trauma-Informed Education

Norton Series on Equity and Social Justice in Education

Cheryl E. Matias and Paul C. Gorski, series editors

Norton's Equity and Social Justice in Education series is a publishing home for books that apply critical and transformative equity and social justice theories to the work of on-the-ground educators. Books in the series describe meaningful solutions to the racism, white supremacy, economic injustice, sexism, heterosexism, transphobia, ableism, neoliberalism, and other oppressive conditions that pervade schools and school districts.

Equity-Centered Trauma-Informed Education
Alex Shevrin Venet

Norton Books in Education

Equity-Centered Trauma-Informed Education

Alex Shevrin Venet

W. W. NORTON & COMPANY
Independent Publishers Since 1923

This work is intended as a general information resource for teachers and school administrators. For case-specific questions and guidance in trauma interventions, please consult with your school and/or community mental-health clinicians. The names of all classroom teachers, students and parents have been changed and identifying details changed or omitted, and many students described in the examples are composites.

Any URLs displayed in this book link or refer to websites that existed as of press time. The publisher is not responsible for, and should not be deemed to endorse or recommend, any website other than its own or any content not created by it. The author, also, is not responsible for any third-party material.

For information about permission to reproduce selections from this book, write to Permissions, W. W. Norton & Company, Inc., 500 Fifth Avenue, New York, NY 10110

For information about special discounts for bulk purchases, please contact W. W. Norton Special Sales at specialsales@wwnorton.com or 800-233-4830

Manufacturing by Versa Press
Book design by Vicki Fischman
Production manager: Katelyn MacKenzie

Library of Congress Cataloging-in-Publication Data

Names: Venet, Alex Shevrin, author.
Title: Equity-centered trauma-informed education / Alex Shevrin Venet.
Description: First edition. | New York : W.W. Norton & Company, 2021. |
Series: Equity & social justice in education series |
Includes bibliographical references and index.
Identifiers: LCCN 2020047256 | ISBN 9780393714739 (paperback) |
ISBN 9780393714746 (epub)
Subjects: LCSH: Children with mental disabilities--Education. |
Psychic trauma in children. | Psychic trauma in adolescence. |
School environment--Psychological aspects.
Classification: LCC LC4601 .V457 2021 | DDC 371.92--dc23
LC record available at https://lccn.loc.gov/2020047256

W. W. Norton & Company, Inc., 500 Fifth Avenue, New York, N.Y. 10110
www.wwnorton.com

W. W. Norton & Company Ltd., 15 Carlisle Street, London W1D 3BS

2 3 4 5 6 7 8 9 0

For my mother

Contents

Part IV
Shift 3: Move From Mindset to Systems Change 123

Part V
Shift 4: Change the World From Inside
Your Classroom 157

Acknowledgments

Writing this book was a solo project, but I never felt alone thanks to the wonderful community of writers, friends, and educators who supported me. I am deeply grateful to all those who offered me feedback on large and small sections of this book: Jenn Baudreau, Jenn Binis, Althea Beagley, Douglas Beagley, Christie Nold, Benjamin Doxtdator, Dana Visser, Ellen O'Neil, Kaitlin Popliearz, Mathew Portell, and especially Sheila Roberts-Veatch and Marian Dingle. Thank you to Anne Schwartz and others who answered #didyouwritetoday? And a big thank you to Paul Gorski and Carol Collins for this opportunity and for your support, feedback, and guidance.

I'm indebted to the educators who are my thought partners and collaborators in pursuit of equity-centered trauma-informed practice. To the brain trust, thank you for pushing my thinking and being a support network. Arlène Casimir, Colleen Wilkinson, and Rhiannon Kim, you make me better. Dulce-Marie Flecha, you have shaped so much of my thinking, and I'm grateful for your friendship. Addison Duane, I truly could not have written this book without you. Your support, encouragement, research help, and friendship are blessings.

Katie E. Decker and Laura Thomas: thank you for the mentorship that has sustained me over the years. I've learned so much from you and from trying to be like you, and I hope this book makes you proud. Thank you. I am also forever grateful to the staff and students at Centerpoint, past, present, and future. You all taught me the meaning of unconditional positive regard.

Thank you to my family and its many branches: Shevrin, Glass, Snyder, Venet, and Perrelli. To Brian, Jason, and especially my dad, Phil, thank you for believing in me and cheering me on. To Nate, thank you for giving me the time, space, love, and steady foundation I needed to write this book, not to mention the sour candy and fixing the printer. I love you and Charlie too.

Introduction

It's the early 1960s in Rochester, New York, and an elementary school girl named Gini sits in class, hoping that no one will notice she's not okay. Gini is one of three children in a seemingly typical white, working-class family. Gini is a star student at her Catholic school and doesn't get in trouble. She overachieves in her classes and gets involved in academic extracurriculars. To all outward appearances, Gini looks like the perfect student from a good family.

Appearances can be deceiving. At home, Gini and her siblings attempt to parent themselves. Their mother is diagnosed with paranoid schizophrenia, and treatments are experimental and largely ineffective. Her erratic behavior is, at best, confusing and, in the worst moments, violent. Gini's father makes himself scarce between constant work and alcohol.

Gini learns that, to survive at school and at home, it serves her well to try to be perfect. Mistakes could trigger her mother's paranoid ranting. Academic achievement and extracurriculars allow Gini to spend more time at school (and less at home). Perfection provides a way to stay under the radar, to not be seen—and, consequently, not be helped.

As an adult, my mother, Gini, rarely talked about her childhood. One notable exception was in a talk she gave to her synagogue in 2012, part of an event aimed at reducing stigma about mental health issues. In her speech, she reflected: "As an adult looking back, I am struck by the fact that none of my teachers ever addressed my situation at home, even on the day that my mother appeared at my elementary school in the midst of a psychotic episode. Nothing was said to me, no advice ever offered. The stigma was too much." Half a century later, how many children still go unheard because the stigma remains?

Childhood trauma does not guarantee a life of failure and struggle. My mother earned degrees in high school, college, and graduate school. She had a successful career in technology, long before women were welcome in that field. She and my dad raised me and my two brothers, providing us a loving and safe home. Nevertheless, she was changed and shaped by the events of her childhood.

Trauma Matters

When my mother was in school, the prevailing wisdom about child trauma was, "Kids are resilient. They'll get over it." Kids *are* resilient, but now we know that "just get over it" isn't the right attitude. We know more about trauma, thanks to the advocacy of trauma survivors and activists and the work of care providers and researchers across many fields: medicine, education, psychology, sociology, and more.

Here's some of what we know. About half of all children in the United States will experience at least one potentially traumatic event before age 18. This number is higher for children of color, especially Black and Latinx children, and children with disabilities are four times more likely to be maltreated (Sacks & Murphey, 2018; Thomas-Skaf & Jenney, 2020). It's challenging to get an accurate sense of the problem because child trauma is hard to measure. Many types of child trauma and abuse happen behind closed doors. Children are threatened or coerced to keep silent, so they do not report what has happened to them. Numbers about child trauma can also be misleading because children can be exposed to several types of adversity (polyvictimization) or not know to identify an experience as traumatic (Saunders & Adams, 2014). Outside of individual events, children can be exposed to trauma through community factors and conditions, such as the ongoing stress of living in poverty. As I wrote this book, the COVID-19 pandemic spread around the globe. Time will tell how an experience of global crisis affects the children who lived through it.

For some children, stress does not become trauma. While some point to "resilience" as a strength or an asset of individual children, the research on resilience takes a more ecological approach in which a child's capacity to respond to challenges is supported by interlocking systems like family, community, and access to resources (Masten, 2018). Children with access to that supportive community are more likely to recover from stress and not experience lasting challenges. For other children, their response to threat and danger causes enduring negative psychological, physical, and spiritual harm. This response is called trauma, and it captures a wide range of effects that vary person to person.

The current consensus also says that no amount of just "pushing past it" helps people heal from trauma. To recover from trauma, we first need to reestablish a feeling of safety, emotionally and psychologically. From there, the journey is different for everyone, but we all need trusted people with whom to build relationships. We need unconditional acceptance. While trauma therapists are one possible source of support, experts in the field emphasize that healing from trauma requires a community that cares, rather than simply 50 minutes a week in a therapist's office (Perry & Szalavitz, 2017; Herman, 1992/2015). Teachers, coaches, neighbors, family, and friends are just some of the members of a child's community of care.

Perhaps the teachers at my mother's school assumed that help would come from outside of their walls, or that their students could simply leave their trauma at the door. In our schools today, we can't make these assumptions. We have children in our care who are struggling with past or ongoing trauma. We are also responsible for the operation of schools that can become traumatic environments for children with otherwise supportive and safe home lives. I don't love when people use the phrase "now more than ever," because our attention to our students' well-being has always been important. So instead I say *now, as ever,* we must commit to creating trauma-informed environments for all our students.

I didn't become a teacher because of my mother's story. There are some pieces of my mother's childhood I learned only about after she gave that 2012 speech. But when I did become a teacher, I took a job at a therapeutic school where most of the students had experienced trauma. My role was "counseling teacher," and I was cross-trained by clinical and educational staff to provide both academic and therapeutic support to our students. I eventually became a school leader there. Within this setting, I was part of a community dedicated to creating better outcomes for our trauma-affected students. As an alternative school, we strove not to recreate the norms of public school in a smaller setting but instead to build a new way of "doing school" from the ground up, with the needs of our students at the center. We made every decision about our school's operation with care and intention, from the design of our classrooms to how we served lunch, as well as the common language we used with students and one another. The mission of our school was grounded in unconditional care for our students, and everything we did had to be aligned with that care.

I'm a nerd for all things education, so as the years went on I started going to lots of professional learning conferences, both locally in Vermont and nationally. I started interacting with all kinds of teachers at different grade levels and school settings and with different years of experience. Just like that, the alternative-school bubble I'd been living in popped and I saw that how we operated in our little school was pretty far from the norm. In my conversations at conferences and online, I observed that many public school teachers were holding on to the same attitudes and beliefs as my mother's teachers from decades ago. These teachers saw the effects of trauma on their students but told me that they felt helpless to do anything about it. I knew the same things that worked well at our small independent school could be of value to teachers in any setting.

It's become my mission to help teachers understand what I learned working at a therapeutic school: that school can be a site of growth and support for students surviving the most challenging circumstances; that school can be structured in intentional ways to promote this growth; and that, together, educators can advocate for systems change that addresses and prevents trauma. We can't single-handedly end all of the complex reasons that trauma occurs from within our classrooms. But we can do more than we realize.

Trauma-Informed Education:
A Healing Force or a Buzzword?

Trauma-informed education is at a crossroads. It has gained enough popularity to be featured by Oprah and to be mentioned by presidential candidates in their education plans. Most educators understand that childhood trauma is far too common, and almost everywhere I go I hear teachers say that they are struggling to meet the needs of their trauma-affected students.

Despite the urgent need, not many schools have fully incorporated an understanding of trauma into practices or policies. There are few examples of what a fully trauma-informed school, district, or system might look like. In academic research individual programs and practices have been studied, but there is a gap in identifying powerful and effective whole-school approaches (Stratford et al., 2020). Schools are engaged in a trial-and-error process as they implement trauma-informed practices, leading to wonderful gains in some places and missing the mark in others.

All this trial and error has education leaders wondering whether trauma-informed practices are helping or hurting. Some of the strongest critiques have come from advocates for educational equity who wonder if "trauma-informed" is just another distraction for schools avoiding the larger work of equity, such as ending racism within schools (Gorski, 2019). Indeed, I have observed firsthand that some schools proudly claim to be working on becoming trauma-informed but refuse to engage in discussions about equity, especially as it connects to racism. Why is trauma-informed education an appealing topic for professional development, but ending the things that *cause* trauma is not?

Advocates of trauma-informed education must listen and truly grapple with these questions. There is a legitimate risk that trauma-informed education becomes a deficit model, used to label and marginalize students who are already marginalized based on their identities. When schools start identifying practices just for the "trauma kids," or assign students a number based on their traumatic experiences, we have lost sight of what's important and have started doing harm. If this is the reality of trauma-informed implementation, it should rightfully pass by as just another educational buzzword. If schools focus on the impacts of trauma that they think they see and not on the inequitable conditions within schools that cause, exacerbate, or perpetuate trauma, then the promise of a trauma-informed approach has failed.

So where do we go from here? Should we abandon this frame because of its potential to do harm? I don't think so. It has been more than a decade since I first started using trauma-informed practices, and I still think they are an essential tool for all schools to work toward equity and justice. I believe in the power of trauma-informed practices to transform our educational system and create a better world. This happens when we see trauma-informed education as inextricably linked to equity and social justice. I believe that this transformation is possible, but only if advocates of trauma-informed education commit to redefining our field.

Book Overview

In this book, I highlight the power of trauma-informed practices to guide our journey toward more equitable and just schools while also cautioning against potential missteps that may sidetrack or weaken our work. My hope for you as the reader is that you will finish this book with a more complex understanding of trauma-informed education and a drive to bring your own trauma-informed work to the next level, with equity at the center.

It is important to note that this book is not meant as a "Trauma 101" text. I hope that you will be familiar with some basic information about what trauma is and how it impacts students in school before you read, because I don't give a full accounting in these pages of the neurobiology of trauma, for example, or strategies for trauma-informed behavior intervention. I regularly update my website (unconditional-learning.org) with current resources, and I recommend the National Child Traumatic Stress Network (NCTSN.org) as a great resource for building your understanding of child trauma. I do review key concepts and definitions in Chapter 1.

This book is also not a guide to trauma-*specific* interventions or counseling approaches. I am not a counselor or a licensed mental health practitioner—I'm a teacher. My suggestions in this book are from the perspective of a teacher and focus on practices for nonclinical teachers and other school staff. As I will mention a few times, it is best practice to consult with your school and community mental health clinicians with case-specific questions or guidance for students impacted by trauma.

So what can you expect from this book instead? I bring my perspective as a teacher and education leader to critically examine how schools need to transform so we can respond to and prevent trauma. I draw on my experience teaching middle and high school, teaching in community college, consulting with K–12 schools, and as a school leader in a small school. Throughout the book I include composite case examples (with names and small details changed or invented) to illustrate what trauma-informed practices look like in the classroom or to demonstrate the impact when these practices are missing. From my experience as a professional development facilitator and teacher educator, I tie together education research, philosophy, and rubber-meets-the-road strategies. I hope that you will be able to quickly implement some of the suggestions in this book while recognizing that others will take groundwork, time, and organizing. Although many books about trauma-informed education focus on the challenging behavior of students, this book mainly addresses the challenging behavior of the *adults* in a school. Therefore, I also hope that you will engage in self-reflection and conversation with colleagues. Equity-centered trauma-informed education is largely about the work of adults in a school, and my hope for readers is that you will use this book as a guide for getting to work.

There are five parts to this book. Part I focuses on bringing equity to the center of trauma-informed education. In Chapter 1 I propose an expanded definition for trauma-informed practices, along with six principles for making trauma-informed education equity centered. Chapter 2 is a deeper dive into the meaning of equity, and I focus on two key connections between equity and trauma: first, inequity causes trauma; second, school isn't equitable for trauma-affected students. Given the links between equity and trauma-informed education, I propose four shifts to move schools closer to an equity-centered trauma-informed environment. Each of the next four parts of the book focuses on one of these shifts.

Part II is about the universal, proactive implementation of trauma-informed practices. In Chapter 3, I examine the adverse childhood experiences (ACEs) framework. Because this framework is so popular and commonly discussed in texts on trauma-informed education, it is important to understand some of the nuances of the ACE checklist and what they mean for universal implementation. Chapter 4 expands on humanization as the core of a universal approach and some of the ways we can ensure that universal interventions are helpful and not harmful. Chapter 5 introduces four proactive priorities to help equity-centered trauma-informed educators infuse an understanding of trauma into our decision making.

The second shift, explored in Part III, is all about relationships. Chapters 6, 7, and 8 dive into the philosophy of unconditional positive regard, with attention to boundaries and ensuring that as teachers we do not position ourselves as saviors. There is a fine line between wanting to help and wanting to rescue, and I invite readers into reflection as they walk this line.

In Part IV, it's time to have a conversation with school leaders. Chapters 9, 10, and 11 are for all educators, but I give special attention to how school leaders must support equity-centered trauma-informed schools. Chapter 11, for example, is about school policy. That may not sound very exciting to teachers, but embedding equity-centered trauma-informed principles into school policy can create lasting change.

Finally, Part V looks at how we can create change from inside our classrooms by fostering student activism and leadership. In Chapters 12 and 13 I make a case for critical pedagogy as trauma-informed pedagogy and invite teachers to think about how we can create healing spaces. Then I conclude by offering some questions to help you shape your own dreams for trauma-informed education in your unique communities.

I am inspired to advocate for trauma-informed practices by my mother's story, but also by the collective story of so many students, teachers, and community advocates who see the potential in schools to disrupt trauma. This book is for all of them: those whose stories we know and those whose stories we don't.

Equity-Centered Trauma-Informed Education

Part I

Bringing Equity to the Center

The trauma-informed education movement is gaining popularity among schools that want to become more supportive of trauma-affected children. But too often trauma-informed practices are considered a separate initiative from a school's efforts to create educational equity. It's time to change that. Equity-centered trauma-informed education is more than adding together existing trauma-informed education and equity initiatives. Instead, equity-centered trauma-informed education is an integrated and holistic approach.

In Part I, I define what it means to be trauma-informed, what it means to be equity-centered, and what is possible at the intersection of the two. Chapter 1 makes the case for the blending of equity work and trauma-informed practice, and describes the principles of equity-centered trauma-informed education. Chapter 2 explores two aspects of the equity and trauma intersection: how inequity creates trauma, and how trauma-affected students experience inequity in school. These chapters also define key terms and build the foundation for the shifts described in the rest of the book.

1 | Defining Trauma-Informed Education

My younger brother works in organic farming. After a few years as a worker on a community-supported vegetable farm, he transitioned into a role helping farmers to achieve organic certification. When he told me about this new role, I admit that I thought to myself: "How hard can certification be? Doesn't 'organic' just mean 'don't use pesticides'?"

I was woefully underinformed about what it means to run an organic farm. It turns out, organic farming goes way beyond whether the tomato I buy at the market is covered in pesticide spray. As my brother explained to me, organic farming is about a system that respects biodiversity, stewardship of the land, and health for humans, soil, plants, and animals. To maintain an organic farm, farmers must foster healthy soil. They need to let fields rest, rather than depleting nutrients every growing season. They must provide areas of wildlife refuge on their farms to maintain biodiversity. In other words, most people understand "organic" as simply a way to differentiate one tomato from the other at the grocery store. But organic farming is truly a systemic approach, based on a value system about respecting and sustaining our natural environment.

As an educator and an advocate for trauma-informed practices, I can relate to my brother's frustration with the public's lack of understanding of what he does. When I mention the words *trauma-informed* to people unfamiliar with the concept, I often hear responses like, "Yeah, those trauma kids need more help," or "Is that when you have a calm-down corner?" Like the grocery shopper comparing tomatoes, all too often we see only the surface-level characterization and not the system of values and beliefs underneath.

Yet the values and beliefs behind trauma-informed practice are essential to articulate. What are we trying to accomplish, and why? In this chapter I answer these questions, both exploring trauma-informed education as it is widely practiced and providing a new definition for moving equity to the center of trauma-informed education.

Narrow Definitions

What is trauma-informed education? This should be easy to answer. After all, trauma-informed education is a hot topic for educators as they attempt to address the needs of students in a traumatic world. But there is no universally agreed-upon definition of trauma-informed education (Thomas et al., 2019; Stratford et al., 2020). The good news: no one company or individual "owns" trauma-informed practices. The bad news is that, in conversations about trauma-informed education, we are not always talking about the same thing.

There are some common threads. Let's look at three definitions of trauma-informed practice:

- In Jim Sporleder and Heather T. Forbes's book *The Trauma-Informed School* (2016), *trauma-informed* "refers to all of the ways in which a service system is influenced by having an understanding of trauma and the ways in which it is modified to be responsive to the impact of traumatic stress" (p. 33).
- Susan E. Craig, author of *Trauma-Sensitive Schools* (2016), wrote that the term *trauma-sensitive schools* "describe[s] the school climate, instructional designs, positive behavioral supports, and policies traumatized students need to achieve academic and social competence" (p. 9).

- According to the Substance Abuse and Mental Health Administration, a trauma-informed approach "realizes the widespread impact of trauma and understands potential paths for recovery; recognizes the signs and symptoms of trauma in clients, families, staff, and others involved with the system; and responds by fully integrating knowledge about trauma into policies, procedures, and practices, and seeks to actively resist re-traumatization" (2014, p. 27).

These definitions, and ones like them, share something in common: they focus on meeting the needs of students *already* impacted by trauma. As an educator who has been implementing trauma-informed practices for over a decade, I think we need a shift. I agree that we need a great deal of change in our education system to better support students impacted by trauma—but this is not enough. One of the limitations of definitions like these is that they imply our role in schools is to address the *impact* of trauma without addressing the *causes* of trauma. They suggest that we can help students who struggle with trauma but that we can't do much about the fact that trauma happens in the first place. I disagree.

To understand this disagreement, we have to look at how educators usually define trauma. Too often, teachers perceive trauma as something that comes from "outside of school." They point to events in the home or place the blame for trauma on neglectful parents. Many education texts on trauma rely on an outdated definition that trauma is caused only by interpersonal violence, such as child abuse or assault, or by big, one-time tragedies, such as terrorism or natural disasters. Trauma is often framed as "all about the brain," and education-focused texts emphasize behavioral impacts of trauma—it's not unusual to see "trauma" and "challenging behavior" go hand in hand. In short, much of the research and writing on trauma frame it as an individual experience, resulting from factors schools cannot control. When we accept that definition, what is our role as educators? To respond to trauma and to mitigate its effects on learning.

But this isn't the only way to understand trauma. Let's look at what we know about trauma and then consider how it plays out in schools.

Adding Complexity

Trauma is a complex concept, with no simple definitions. Literacy professor Elizabeth Dutro, who focuses on trauma and literacy, has cautioned educators to resist oversimplifications and the use of *trauma* as a label to sort and categorize children: "[*Trauma*] is not a word to be used lightly, to toss around" (2017, p. 327). I second Dutro's caution and also recognize that we need some common language to talk about trauma. Therefore, consider the information in the text box as a snapshot of a moving object, and recognize that understandings of trauma continue to expand and evolve.

TRAUMA: A FEW BASICS
What Is Trauma?

Trauma can be both an individual and collective response to life-threatening events, harmful conditions, or a prolonged dangerous or stressful environment. Not all stressful experiences are traumatic to individuals. For those who do develop a trauma response, the impact can be intense, pervasive, and disruptive, affecting both the mind and the body.

Trauma and *posttraumatic stress disorder* are not interchangeable terms. Posttraumatic stress disorder (PTSD) is defined by a specific set of symptoms identified by psychologists, but not all people who experience trauma will be diagnosed with PTSD, and not all indicators of trauma align with PTSD symptoms. A more expansive definition of trauma goes beyond a pathological/medical definition and understands trauma as a collective and sociopolitical concept.

What Types of Events or Conditions Cause Trauma?

Judith L. Herman, a leading voice in the literature on trauma, wrote that "traumatic events are extraordinary, not because they occur rarely, but rather because they overwhelm the ordinary human adaptations to life" (1992/2015, p. 33). The modern concept of trauma was developed through the activism of Vietnam War veterans and women survivors of domestic violence (Herman, 1992/2015; Van der Kolk, 2015).

Since that initial wave of activism and research, our understanding of trauma has expanded greatly, and it is now recognized that many types of events and circumstances can cause a traumatic response, including abuse, neglect, bullying, racism, natural disasters, and more.

Trauma can also be understood from a collective lens, as when a community undergoes a shared trauma (e.g., the Jewish community and the Holocaust). Historical trauma refers to the collective impact of trauma throughout generations (Brave Heart et al., 2011). And we can also understand trauma as an ongoing environment. Educator and healing justice advocate Shawn A. Ginwright (2016, p. 3) has pointed out that for many youth of color there is no "post" as in posttraumatic stress disorder; instead they experience a persistent traumatic stress environment.

Who Experiences Trauma?

Anyone can experience trauma. Researchers estimate that between half and three-quarters of all children will experience a potentially traumatic event prior to age 18. Whether or not a specific child experiences an event or condition as traumatic depends on many factors, including age, temperament, social support systems, and the intensity and duration of the event or condition. Protective factors that buffer the effects of trauma include a strong community support system and relationships with reliable adults and caregivers (National Child Traumatic Stress Network, 2012; Masten 2018).

How Does Trauma Impact a Child?

Trauma affects everyone differently. The stress of a trauma response can impact our minds and bodies. Symptoms of a trauma response can include depression, anxiety, anger, aggression, hypervigilance, physiological changes such as disrupted sleep or appetite, and more. Trauma research groups like the Child Trauma Academy (https://www .childtrauma.org/) are studying how the timing and duration of early-life stress can impact cognitive and social functioning, as well as how social connections mediate these effects. The impacts of trauma can also be invisible to others or delayed until adulthood.

A Structural Lens

In expanding our definitions of trauma, we must make sure we see trauma as a structural issue, not just an individual one. Scholars now recognize what people from marginalized communities have always known: oppression, bias, and discrimination cause trauma (Haines, 2019; Becker-Blease, 2017; Khasnabis & Goldin, 2020). Racism causes trauma. Islamophobia causes trauma. Heterosexism causes trauma. Transphobia causes trauma. And I'm not just talking about visible incidences of hate crimes. Oppression causes trauma through the ways it is built into the everyday structures of school and society and how these structures have persisted throughout generations. Trauma doesn't just happen at home—students can be traumatized by conditions and events in schools, and schools can cause trauma (I unpack this idea fully in Chapter 2). And trauma's effects can be passed down through generations and spread through communities.

In schools, a structural lens means that we stop seeing trauma as a problem affecting only certain children. Instead, we start recognizing the role that schools have to play in causing and worsening trauma because of the role of schools in perpetuating oppression. Most professional development about trauma-informed education addresses only the individual nature of trauma, providing tips about how to support students who are stressed because of adversity. This would lead us to believe that we are trauma-informed if we provide students with caring teachers, flexible academic structures, and counseling, or if we change our approach to classroom management. These are important considerations, but trauma-informed solutions need to address not just these individual students but also the structures, systems, and inequalities that cause trauma (Khasnabis & Goldin, 2020). For example, a student is bullied for being poorer than her classmates. Typical trauma-informed education suggestions would be to intervene with the student's classmates to stop the bullying and then provide support to the affected student. This might look like inviting her to a lunch bunch to build positive social connections or teaching her self-regulation skills to manage her distress. These are necessary first steps. But those interventions address only the individual causes of the student's trauma. We also have to ask: What were the conditions in our school that created the bullying in the first place? How do our students understand one another's relative incomes and family structures? How might school be contributing to inequities between students or drawing attention to poverty? What are we doing to help students and families access resources? By focusing only on the student's coping skills, we may be sending the message that it's more important to cope with your own marginalization than to work to end the factors that are marginalizing you. As educators Debi Khasnabis and Simon Goldin wrote, "Treating trauma *only* as an individual-level problem, when it is not, has the unfortunate and perhaps somewhat predictable effect of blaming children and families for challenges they did not cause" (2020, p. 46).

Schools can also contribute to the larger social conditions that cause trauma. A student is sexually assaulted by her boyfriend over the weekend. Is the school responsible? That specific school may not be, but in a broader sense schools are social institutions and one of the primary places where children learn about social norms. Sexual assault against women and girls is not a collection of individual acts made by individual boys and men. Instead, sexual violence is understood as existing within a culture that normalizes male violence and sexualizes young girls. Schools are responsible for their role in either actively disrupting these messages or allowing them to perpetuate. If a school provides support for a sexual violence survivor but also refuses to teach comprehensive sex education, can we call that school trauma-informed?

A New Definition

With our expanded understanding of trauma comes an expanded role that educators can play. When we recognize that trauma originates from both inside and outside of schools, we realize that it is not simply our job to respond to trauma or to reduce potential triggers inside of school. Instead, we become key agents in ending the trauma that happens within our schools and our education system. When we recognize that social, historical, and political factors shape trauma, we can imagine ways that schools can influence these factors in pursuit of a better world.

To reflect this expanded role, I propose a new definition for trauma-informed education:

> Trauma-informed educational practices respond to the impacts
> of trauma on the entire school community and prevent future
> trauma from occurring. Equity and social justice are key concerns
> of trauma-informed educators as we make changes in our
> individual practice, in classrooms, in schools, and in district-wide
> and state-wide systems.

In a trauma-informed approach, we use our understanding of trauma and its impact on children to shift our approach to education in classrooms, schools, and broader systems. This transformation is not straightforward. In learning more about trauma, it has become clear to me that our current educational system is not set up with the needs of trauma survivors in mind. Worse, school systems and individual educators can be the *perpetrators* of trauma. A trauma-informed lens requires that we also critically think about the status quo in education and be willing to make significant changes to the ways we do things.

This expanded definition reflects our hopes for trauma-informed education to be more than a response to challenging student behavior. Educators Shantel D. Crosby, Penny Howell, and Shelly Thomas wrote about the potential for trauma-informed teaching to advance social justice: "Rather than blaming and punishing students for their reactions to their circumstances, trauma-informed teaching has an embedded social justice perspective that seeks to disassemble oppressive systems within the school" (2018, p. 20). This *embedded* perspective needs to be highlighted every time we talk about trauma-informed education, so we never lose our focus.

(A note on language: Throughout this book I use *trauma-informed education* and *trauma-informed practices* interchangeably to refer to *trauma-informed educational practices*).

Shifting Equity to the Center

At the heart of the new definition of trauma-informed practice is a focus on equity. Simply put, *educational equity* is the work of ensuring that all students have access to a high-quality education and the resources they need to be successful in school. (Chapter 2 does a deeper dive into defining equity and the connections to trauma-informed practice.) Equity is sometimes understood as a component of social justice. In this book I use *social justice* to refer to the larger task of addressing and ending oppression in the world, and I use *equity* to refer to this work in the context of school.

To understand why we need to focus on equity, we first must acknowledge that our current education system in the United States is not (and has never been) equitable. While our system is supposed to serve all students, the reality is that many students are left behind and pushed out through no fault of their own. For example, students who live in high-poverty areas usually attend schools with far less funding, and lower school funding typically leads to worse school outcomes for students (Semuels, 2016). School funding is not in the control of any student, yet students' futures are affected by this inequitable allocation of resources.

In Chapter 2 I explain that inequity in schools can cause or worsen trauma. Yet, too often, trauma-informed education is considered separately from equity concerns. For example, many trauma-informed texts recommend that teachers collaborate with school counselors. Yet almost one in five students does not have access to a school counselor at all, and students of color and poor students are less likely to have access to a counselor (Education Trust & Cratty, 2019). Lack of counseling support in school is an equity issue, and if we merely say "be more trauma informed" without addressing the larger equity issue, we are missing a big part of the picture. This is just one example of many that speak to the need for bringing equity to the center.

So where is equity now, if not in the center?

- *On the side:* Equity work is often relegated to a committee that meets only a few times a year and spends more time studying equity than taking action to bring it about.
- *Underground:* Equity work is taken up by only a few teachers, often teachers of color, who implement antiracist and other equity-focused practices behind closed doors for fear of rocking the boat.

- *In the ether:* Equity work is talked about only in the abstract or used as a buzzword in the school's mission statement. No one ever actually talks about what inequity looks like, concretely and at their own school, or how to fix it.
- *Nowhere:* In too many schools equity is never talked about at all.

With the knowledge that inequities contribute to trauma, equity needs to be at the center of trauma-informed practices. This means that conversations about instructional design, social-emotional learning, sports, and even the cafeteria include equity considerations. Equity at the center means always asking, Does this practice, policy, or decision help or harm students from marginalized communities? Because the same factors that cause inequity (e.g., bias and discrimination) also cause trauma, we can't unlink the two.

I've read too many books on trauma-informed practice that fail to mention race in more than a passing way or that ignore the reality that systemic issues contribute to trauma. I've visited (and worked in) too many schools where administrators say "we're trauma informed" but refuse to address the equity issues that students and teachers say are harming them. In a research review of 20 years of studies related to trauma-informed education, Adam Alvarez found that researchers tended to ignore or minimize issues of race and racial equity in their work: "Trauma may be one of the most underexplored racial equity issues in education" (2020, p. 31). We show our values through what we choose to include. It's time to stop excluding equity from our visions for trauma-informed schools.

My goal in this book is to help educators and education leaders build a vision of equity-centered trauma-informed schools. This means that schools are *informed* by an understanding of trauma, both *responding* to the impact of trauma on the school community and *preventing* trauma at school. These schools also place equity at the center instead of treating it as an initiative or an extra.

This vision of equity-centered trauma-informed schools is based on six principles. Table 1.1 describes each of these principles, along with the key understandings on which they are based and the steps equity-centered trauma-informed schools can take to put the principles into action.

Table 1.1: Principles of Equity-Centered Trauma-Informed Education	
Principle 1: Antiracist, antioppression—Trauma-informed education is antiracist and against all forms of oppression.	**Key understanding:** Racism, sexism, homophobia, classism, transphobia, and all forms of oppression *cause* trauma. Inequity in schools causes trauma. **Task of equity-centered trauma-informed education:** Begin by examining and understanding how oppression harms students within our schools. End the school conditions and practices that cause trauma.
Principle 2: Asset based—Trauma-informed education is asset based and doesn't attempt to fix kids, because kids are not broken. Instead, it addresses the conditions, systems, and structures that harm kids.	**Key understanding:** Children have an inherent capacity to survive, thrive, and heal. Trauma is a normal response to threat, so there's nothing to fix about trauma-affected children. Instead, we fix the inequities that cause and worsen trauma, and we build systems of support. **Task of equity-centered trauma-informed education:** Create equitable school environments that are safe and affirming. Rid ourselves of any savior mentality that causes us to discount the agency and self-determination of students.
Principle 3: Systems oriented—Trauma-informed education is a full ecosystem, not a list of strategies.	**Key understanding:** Classroom practice, institutional culture and norms, and systems-level policy are all interconnected, and sustained equity requires change at all levels. Students need an entire trauma-informed environment, not just a trauma-informed teacher. **Task of equity-centered trauma-informed education:** Implement trauma-informed practices across an entire school, as well as district-wide and state-wide education systems. Change policy as well as classroom practice.

Principle 4: Human centered—Trauma-informed education means centering our shared humanity.	**Key understanding:** Dehumanization causes trauma. Educational equity isn't actually equity if it rests on dehumanizing attitudes and policies. Healing requires being fully human, with all of the mess and complexity that entails. Standardization and depersonalization are antithetical to human-centered education.
	Task of equity-centered trauma-informed education: Rid schools of dehumanizing practices and policies. Resist one-size-fits-all and zero-tolerance approaches. Don't allow a focus on the trauma to cause us to lose sight of the person.
Principle 5: Universal and proactive—Trauma-informed education is a universal approach, implemented proactively.	**Key understanding:** Identifying and labeling "trauma kids" causes inequity and creates further marginalization. Trauma-informed practices benefit all students, and the best time to implement them is before trauma has occurred.
	Task of equity-centered trauma-informed education: Don't wait for a tragedy to provide trauma-informed education. Avoid approaches that label or sort children. Pair proactive strategies with responsive supports, and eliminate barriers to access.
Principle 6: Social justice focused—Trauma-informed education aims to create a trauma-free world.	**Key understanding:** Responding to trauma that has already happened isn't enough. Ending current harm is a good first step. The ultimate goal of trauma-informed education is to not need trauma-informed education.
	Task of equity-centered trauma-informed education: Don't view equity and social justice as strategies to reduce disparities or lower suspension rates. Instead, keep perspective on the larger goal of creating a more just world and working for collective liberation from oppression.

The Four Shifts We Need

How do we move from the schools we have today to the schools that are fully trauma-informed and equity-centered? One approach is "burn it all down and start over," and in some ways I'm a proponent of that approach. Some schools and, more broadly, some education practices are so harmful that no amount of tinkering can fix them. For example, simply tweaking the funding in a school that has been underfunded, poorly maintained, and segregated for generations isn't likely to make impactful change. For this reason, many education activists have called for abolition of the current system and rebuilding a new one (see, e.g., Love, 2019). Others see the potential in making a transformation within our current education landscape.

However you approach school change, I hope this book gives you some places to start the transformation. In Parts II–V I describe four shifts that bring us from a traditional approach to school, where trauma-informed practice is an add-on and equity is on the side, to a more integrated approach where *equity-centered trauma-informed* is a lens informing every aspect of our work:

1. Shift from a reactive stance, in which we identify who has been traumatized and support them, to a proactive approach. Trauma-informed practices are universal and benefit everyone (Part II).
2. Shift from a savior mentality, in which we see ourselves as rescuing broken kids, to unconditional positive regard, a mindset that focuses on the inherent skills, capacities, and value of every student. Educators shouldn't aim to heal, fix, or save but to be connection makers and just one of many caring adults in a child's life (Part III).
3. Shift from seeing trauma-informed practices as the responsibility of individual teachers to embedding them in the way that we do school, from policies to practice. Trauma-informed teachers need trauma-informed leaders (Part IV).
4. Shift from focusing only on how trauma affects our classroom to seeing how what happens in our classroom can change the world. We can partner with our students as change makers for a more just society (Part V).

I use the pronoun *we* to refer to the larger community of educators but recognize that many teachers and schools already have made at least some of these shifts. Some teachers never needed to make these shifts in the first place because their practice has been grounded in love and liberation from the start. I hope these readers will feel affirmed as they recognize their powerful practices described in these pages.

My definition of equity-centered trauma-informed practice and these four shifts are aspirational. I don't know of any school, program, or individual (not even me) who currently implements trauma-informed practices perfectly, because there is no perfect implementation or checklist to be completed. Instead, trauma-informed practices should evolve continuously as our understanding evolves. These four shifts also don't capture the be-all and end-all of trauma-informed practices. Real change is complicated, messy, and never truly done. Consider these four shifts as a starting place for growing your practice. In redefining trauma-informed practices in education, I hope to help propel this field forward with equity at the center.

Changing Practice, Pedagogy, and Policy

Throughout this book I offer suggestions for transformation across all major aspects of schooling: practice, pedagogy, and policy:

- *Practice:* We need to expand our mindsets. We can sharpen our lens of understanding and apply it to our individual daily practice of interacting with our students and our colleagues. Developing our lens is not simply so we know better but so we are prepared to do better.
- *Pedagogy:* School change happens most immediately in the classroom. We can shift both what we teach and how we teach it. Shifting our mindset isn't enough; we also need to put our understanding into action in our classrooms.
- *Policy:* Schools also have work to do at a systems level. Even if I work hard to change my own mindset and translate that into classroom practice and pedagogy, I'm still just one teacher in a larger school. In turn, my school is just one part of a much bigger system.

School leaders must shift policy and procedures so that there is change that outlives any individual member of a school staff.

These three layers are all important, and an equity-centered trauma-informed approach requires that we learn to be good jugglers of all three at once. It's not enough to simply change our mindset, for example, if we continue teaching in the same way we always have. It's also not enough to transform individual classrooms if the school as a whole is shaped by harmful policies and rules. Becoming an equity-centered trauma-informed school requires that we take action in all three arenas.

We can think about this using the concept of an equity-centered trauma-informed *ecology* (Crosby, 2015). Just like in nature, a healthy ecosystem relies on the interactions among many interwoven elements. An equity-centered teacher needs an equity-centered leader, and they work best together when the policies support their efforts. If any element is out of place, it can be difficult to make progress.

These recommendations are woven through the text. They are also highlighted at the end of most chapters, as action steps that correspond to each of these three areas, to underscore the importance of change at multiple levels within a school system:

- Developing our lens (practice)
- Transforming our classrooms (pedagogy)
- Shifting the larger systems (policy)

I hope you will consider these steps not as a checklist but as a menu. Choose something that you can influence and go from there. The important thing is to begin.

Start Where You Are

Depending on your role in your school and your sphere of influence, you may be wondering how you can make change in the complicated education ecosystem. It's okay to start where you are. It can be tempting to say, "Well, I need to wait until my coworkers are on board," or "I can't do anything until my principal changes how he leads." These are real problems, but there is always a way to begin in our own roles. In her book *Leadership and the New Science* (2006), Margaret Wheatley wrote about making change from within a system:

> *Acting locally allows us to be inside the movement and flow of the system, a participant in all those complex events occurring simultaneously. . . . Activities in one part of the whole create effects that appear in distant places. Because of these unseen connections, there is potential value in working anywhere in the system. We never know how our small activities will affect others through the invisible fabric of our connectedness. (p. 45)*

There is value in all of our work, anywhere in the system. At the same time, it can be pretty darn frustrating to feel like we're doing all of that work and not seeing any of the larger issues go away, year after year.

There comes a point in almost every workshop or graduate course that I facilitate when a teacher raises her hand and says, "You keep talking about this system-wide stuff, but what am I supposed to do in the meantime? I can't change our district policy or the state requirements." I love this question.

In reply, I hold up one hand and say, "There are always going to be actions you can take right now, tomorrow morning in your classroom, that start to make change for your trauma-affected students." Holding up the other hand, I continue, "And then there are the bigger-picture changes that need to happen at the school, district, state, or even national level. There are pieces of our US culture and values that would need to shift for there to be a truly equitable experience for our students." Then, I bring my hands together back to back, rubbing my knuckles together to demonstrate the friction. "What I want is for you to notice that tension and accept that it's there. There are no easy solutions or quick fixes, and you *should* feel frustrated at the size and complexity of the systems that need to change. My life's mission is that, if enough educators feel that friction, we can start a revolution and overthrow the inequitable systems." (I smile when I say that, but I'm not really joking.)

If you are reading this book and you have control and influence over larger pieces of our educational system, I encourage you to use your influence to embed equity and trauma-informed practices into policies and systems. If you're reading this and you're a classroom teacher who feels you have little influence over the big picture, don't feel discouraged. You do have enormous influence in the lives of your students, and as we'll explore throughout this book, those individual relationships matter a great deal.

Start where you are. In this book I point to many inroads for making change. Some will be out of your control, but many will be squarely within your influence. There is value in your work anywhere within our school system as we work for equity-centered trauma-informed change.

ACTION STEPS

The suggested action steps for this chapter focus on creating connections and expanding your understanding about trauma. Partner with students, community groups, and experts to make trauma-informed practices both responsive and proactive.

Develop Your Lens
- Foster connections with local organizations, nonprofits, and community organizers who are working with and for survivors of trauma in your area. This might include youth shelters, community mental health organizations, anti-sexual-violence organizations, or foster agencies. These organizations have institutional knowledge, awareness of resources, and often the ability to provide consultation or support to schools. For example, I knew that a local organization near me had a hotline for people experiencing sexual violence, but I was surprised to learn that teachers could also call the hotline to consult with trained staff about how to support their students when talking about dating violence. This organization also offered training for schools, as well as youth leadership opportunities. Schools can provide stronger support for students when we create connections within our community.

- View yourself as a life-long learner when it comes to trauma. Keep up-to-date on developments in the trauma studies field, resisting static frameworks or remaining stuck on outdated recommendations. In my research for this book I've been fascinated by how much the collective understanding of trauma and trauma-informed practices has changed and evolved even over the past 20 years. You can stay up-to-date through following researchers and authors on Twitter, joining newsletters or Facebook groups focusing on trauma, or subscribing to academic journals.

Transform Your Classroom

- Consider how to incorporate trauma prevention into your curriculum. Connect with your school's health teacher or school counselor about initiatives like bullying prevention, substance use prevention, and relationship violence prevention. Often there are ways to weave these into your academic content: look at the evolution of bullying laws in your state as part of a civics unit, investigate the effects of substances on developing brains in science, or analyze characters in whole-class novels through a lens of healthy and safe relationships. I discuss more about classroom approaches in Part V.

Shift the Systems

- Evaluate your current implementation of trauma-informed practices through the lens of "respond and prevent." Equity-centered trauma-informed practices both respond to trauma that's already happened and prevent future trauma from occurring. If your school is currently implementing trauma-informed practices, make a list of these practices, pedagogical tools, and policy shifts. Then go through your list and mark whether each item responds to students who have already experienced trauma, builds a culture of trauma prevention, or both. What do you notice and wonder about your list?

2 | Defining Equity

Moving equity to the center of our trauma-informed practice requires that we consider two questions: First, how does inequity in school cause or worsen student trauma? Second, is school equitable for students who struggle with the impact of trauma in their lives? In this chapter, I dig into the meaning of educational equity and how it connects to trauma-informed practice.

This chapter expands on Principle 1 of equity-centered trauma-informed education: *Trauma-informed education is antiracist and against all forms of oppression.*

What Is Equity?

All students are capable of learning and should have access to an education that helps them grow and learn. I believe most educators would agree with that statement, but our education system does not currently reflect this shared belief. Individual teachers, administrators, and policy makers regularly make decisions that show we do not truly believe that every student deserves a high-quality education. If we really believe, then why don't we fully fund schools and pay teachers well? If we truly believe, then why would we make some educationally enriching experiences in schools, such as sports and clubs, available only to students whose families can pay expensive fees? If we truly believe in a vision of an enriching and challenging education for all, why does school segregation persist (and worsen) decades after *Brown v. Board of Education*?

The education system is not doing what our students need it to do. This is why we need to put equity at the center of our work.

Educational equity is the process of ensuring that all students can access high-quality education, that they are fully included in their school communities, that they are able to engage in meaningful and challenging academic work, and that they can do all of this in an environment that values them as people. A Black student who gains admission to a rigorous charter school but then is discouraged from enrolling in advanced placement (AP) classes is not experiencing educational equity. Neither is a public school student whose teachers hold high expectations and challenge her in academic courses but who hears racial epithets whispered every time she walks through the hallways. To live out the belief that all students are valued, are capable, and have the right to their education, we need to fight for equity in all aspects of our students' experiences.

The National Equity Project (n.d.) defines equity as all children receiving "what they need to develop to their full academic and social potential." This is not the same thing as equality. If my focus is on equality, I try to treat everyone the same. This sounds good in theory, but the reality is that everyone is not the same, and there are no one-size-fits-all strategies. In the college courses I teach, for example, I generally ask students not to use their cell phones. During one class session I noticed that a student had her phone out and seemed to be texting. Once the class got to work on an individual task, I walked over to her, intending to remind her to put the phone away, but when I got closer I realized that she had a translation app open. This student was not fluent in the English academic terms we were using in class, and she was checking the translations to her first language. If my focus were on equality, I would have told this student that, just like everyone else, she needed to put her phone away. Because my focus is on equity, I encouraged her to keep using the app.

It's not just about individual students, though. Recall from Chapter 1 that we can't just look at the pesticide-free tomato to understand organic farming; we also need to consider the sustainable farming practices. Equity, too, is about creating sustainable change. Equity is working toward justice. If I've helped one student access and experience her education, I'm not done: there need to be systems and conditions that create and sustain equity for all. It's not enough for my student to be allowed to use the translation app; I also need to assess whether I'm using needlessly obscure terms that prevent non-native-English speakers from understanding me. I also need to listen to my multilingual students learning English and find out what they need, both from me and from our college, to be successful. And to focus on justice, I need to consider whether my English-language-learning students are facing bias or discrimination within our school setting, or in our community at large, and work to address those conditions.

When I focus on trauma-informed education with equity at the center, my concern does not center only on the trauma-affected students currently in schools. I'm also concerned about preventing future harm to children and, on a larger scale, interrupting the conditions that cause trauma in the first place. True equity would look like an end to the social injustices and conditions that lead to children being harmed.

Schools cannot accomplish this alone, and indeed, a key piece of equity work is recognizing how systems like schools, health care, and the economy are all interrelated. For example, consistent attendance supports student success. If a student lives in a poorly maintained low-income housing unit, she might get sick from exposure to mold. If her family doesn't have health insurance, she may not be able to get the medical attention she needs to get better, and so her attendance suffers. Punishing the student and her family for truancy doesn't advance educational equity; reducing barriers to safe housing and health care does. These problems are complex and multilayered. How do we cultivate our understanding of these connections? We need to develop equity literacy.

Equity Literacy

To produce one organic tomato, the entire system of an organic farm needs to follow sustainable practices over the course of years. For farmers this can mean learning to farm in a new way and dispensing of harmful practices. A farmer can't just snap his fingers and say, "Now my farm is organic"—it takes time, new knowledge, and skill development to make the change.

Transforming our teaching practices for equity is similar. I can't simply snap my fingers and say, "Now my school is equitable," or "Now I teach in equitable ways." Instead, I need to see my drive for equity as a learning process, and as when learning anything, I need to practice skills and gain knowledge to successfully meet my goals.

Educator, researcher, and author Paul Gorski has offered a framework for teachers striving for equity: equity literacy. Gorski has defined equity literacy as "the knowledge and skills educators need to become a threat to the existence of bias and inequity in our spheres of influence" (2018, p. 17). How do we threaten inequity? Something I love about teachers is that we are fierce advocates. Pretty much every teacher I know has at some point gone to bat for a student who was being treated unfairly, falling through the cracks, or not getting the help they needed. I've seen teachers spend hours researching community supports, making phone calls, and contacting local representatives to get a student appropriate help. To become a threat to inequity, we need to bring this same fire and relentlessness to our work for all students, not just individuals. We need to challenge systems, advocate for resources, and make changes within our schools so that inequity doesn't stand a chance against us.

I am drawn to the equity literacy framework because I'm a teacher, and teachers know that learning is a process. When I work with my students on grammar skills, I know that they won't become perfect users of semicolons with one quick lecture. I know that they need to read a lot of writing with rich and varied language. I know they need time to write and experiment with revisions. I know that they need concepts explained in several ways and guidance and correction from me.

The frame of equity literacy allows us as educators to see our work as a learning process, as well. Reading this book (or any other one book) won't automatically make you an expert on equity issues. You will need practice, coaching, role models, and time. This isn't to say that we should take it slow: our students can't wait for us to become experts before we act. Instead, think of your equity literacy development as an action-research project. Work in continuous cycles: learn to recognize inequity, and then when you see it, challenge it and work to change it. Reflect on the process and continue to grow your competence and skills in working for equity.

Equity and Holding Many Perspectives at Once

An equity approach in schools requires that we look beyond the individual and engage with systemic and structural lenses on education. Like the farmer considering her crops but also the entire food chain, we consider individual students and teachers and also consider social, political, historical, and economic factors. For example, consider a high school in a small city where the student population is about 60% white and 40% Black and Latinx. The enrollment in individual classes should reflect that overall racial breakdown. Yet in the school's AP classes almost all of the students are white, with only a few students of color enrolled in each section. How might you address this situation?

Before we look at solving an inequitable situation, we have to understand why it's happening. And to do that, we have to ask questions on several levels. On the student-focused level, we can look at factors in an individual student's educational history and learning profile. Why are the individual Black and Latinx seniors in a given year not enrolling in AP courses? What was the decision-making process for each of them? At a classroom level, we can examine the academic expectations of teachers and how they support student readiness for advanced courses. For example, did teachers with implicit bias about Black students give those students less rigorous feedback or hold them to lower standards? Were some students "tracked" into lower-level courses based on teacher beliefs about their potential? On a school-wide level, we might ask how school counselors are advising course enrollment, or we might ask how racism is operating within the school. Did counselors guide Latinx students toward more career-focused options rather than college, for example, or are Black students avoiding AP courses because of racist bullying by white peers in those classes?

Our understanding of this problem through an equity lens also includes the political, historical, and economic factors previously mentioned. These questions are big and complex, and it seems that, in attempting to answer just one question, many more arise. How could economic hardship impact a student's ability to be successful in an AP course, and how does historical racism connect to who experiences economic hardship? Why are schools, or some programs within schools, still so segregated when the 1954 Supreme Court decision in *Brown v Board of Education* was supposed to ensure racial integration in schools? What stories are represented in the AP curriculum, and what narratives do those stories tell us about race? Whose perspective is represented? Whose is silenced?

When we consider all of these layers and perspectives together, we start to develop an equity lens through which to see education. With an equity lens, we recognize the many factors that contribute to an individual student's academic success. Looking through this lens, we also come to understand why educational and health disparities are connected to gender, race, class, disability, and other markers of identity and how these disparities are not caused by any deficit with the students themselves.

To continue developing your equity literacy, identify situations like the AP class example and see how many questions you can ask about how this inequity came to exist. Seek out other perspectives and talk about it with colleagues. The more we can regularly learn to see inequity, the more we can take action.

A friend shared a story with me about walking with her adult son in New Orleans. He paused to look at some musicians playing jazz on the street and said, "I always wanted to learn to play the saxophone." My friend was surprised and asked why he never did. Her son reminded her that in elementary school he hadn't met grade-level benchmarks in reading, and only students who met those benchmarks were able to join the band. I wonder about the ripple effects of a decision like this: How much was lost for this student because of the act of being excluded from the arts? Could a successful experience with the arts have elevated his whole academic trajectory? A policy like the one my friend's son experienced is an example of how schools can perpetuate inequity and cause harm.

If we want schools to be trauma-informed, we need to fight for equity, because a lack of equity causes trauma. I believe that schools can be powerful communities for learning, growth, and change. To make this real, we need to be both trauma-informed and equity-centered.

The Equity-Centered Trauma-Informed Connection

Now that we've laid the groundwork for understanding equity, let's turn our focus to the connection and interaction between trauma-informed practices and equity. There are two main things to understand about this intersection: First, inequity in schools can cause and worsen trauma. Second, schools are not set up to be equitable for trauma-affected students. For students who experience trauma, traditional structures of school can be, at best, trauma-indifferent and, at worst, trauma-inducing. If we truly wish to respond to trauma and prevent it, both of these connections should be front and center in our trauma-informed work.

Inequity in Schools Can Cause and Worsen Trauma

When we talk about trauma-informed practices, sometimes I hear the phrase "students bring trauma to school." This statement isn't problematic on the surface. Many students, of course, have hardships outside of school, and that trauma is carried with them. Trauma-informed education should be responsive to the emotional needs of students and not assume that students can leave their problems at the door. Digging a little deeper, the problem with the phrase "bringing trauma to school" is that it seems to imply that trauma *only* happens outside of school.

The idea that trauma only happens in the home or outside of school is implied or stated outright in dozens of books and articles, in conference keynotes, and in tweets and Facebook posts. In an often-recommended text for teachers and administrators, the first "critical step to implementing a trauma-informed school" is to embrace the concept that "the stress is coming from outside of school" (Sporleder & Forbes, 2016, p. 5). The authors recommended the mantra "It's not about me" to internalize this concept. I argue that one of the first steps to implementing a trauma-informed school is that we recognize that stress comes from *inside* of school as well, and that sometimes this truly is about us.

This is the uncomfortable truth: schools cause trauma and harm. Teachers and administrators, as individuals, can perpetrate this harm, such as making derogatory remarks about children's racial identity or family. School systems, such as rules, policies, and procedures, can cause trauma and harm, for example, harsh discipline policies that refer children to the criminal justice system for behavior in school. And students can cause trauma and harm to one another through bullying and harassment, especially when adults allow racism and other oppression to flourish.

This can be painful to reconcile. I believe most educators get into teaching because we care about kids. We want to be part of schools that feel like communities. It's tempting to look at the examples I just mentioned and say, "Well, that doesn't happen in my school," or "I would never cause pain to one of my students." Looking away, however, benefits no one. If we want to create more equitable schools and systems for all students, we need first to reckon with practices and attitudes currently causing harm.

The following three experiences, each common in school settings, illustrate how students can be exposed to extreme stress and danger within schools.

Bullying and Harassment. One potential cause of trauma in schools is the cruelty that sometimes takes place among students. Whether harassment, bullying, or violence, conflict between students in school isn't just "kids being kids." This trauma can have a lasting negative impact on students. Children who are bullied are more likely to develop depression, anxiety, and posttraumatic stress disorder (Moore et al., 2017; Ossa et al., 2019).

What do bullying and other forms of harassment have to do with equity? Not all students are at equal risk for harm from bullying, and bullying can thrive in schools where we don't address discrimination and where we don't intentionally create inclusive and validating communities. LGBTQ students and students with disabilities are more likely to be bullied than their peers (Marsh, 2018). Students of color are more likely to be bullied than their white peers and more likely to be bullied based on race (YouthTruth, 2018). While bullying is sometimes framed as a relational conflict, bullying is about power and must be understood in the context of racism, homophobia, transphobia, and oppression (Haines-Saah et al., 2018). This is why interventions aimed at ending bullying with messages of "be kind" and "don't be a bystander" are mostly ineffective. Instead, what works to decrease bullying is creating equitable, affirming school environments. Our efforts toward equity can help decrease bullying as a potential source of trauma.

The harm that students can do to one another also takes the form of hate and bias incidents. In a Southern Poverty Law Center report titled *Hate at School* (2019), Maureen B. Costello and Coshandra Dillard found that incidents of hate and bias are widespread and seem to be on the rise in an increasingly polarized political climate. The report highlights examples of hate and bias in schools, including racist comments by students to their peers, social media postings of students mimicking a Nazi salute, and teachers dressing in stereotype-laden Halloween costumes as Mexicans with a "build the wall" message. One of the most disturbing findings: school leaders often do nothing to respond to hateful incidents in schools, not even denouncing bias in 9 cases out of 10.

Considering all of this, we can see that students who do not "bring trauma to school" can experience trauma within the school walls. School leaders and teachers, while not wholly responsible for the existence of racism and bias in society, are responsible for how racism and bias are interrupted and dismantled in our schools.

Police and Zero-Tolerance Policies. Given the complex nature of these issues, it may be tempting for school leaders to implement zero-tolerance policies in the name of protecting vulnerable students. Zero-tolerance policies, however, actually harm students, especially Black students and other students of color.

Police and other law enforcement officers assigned to public schools, usually known as school resource officers (SROs), are a common fixture. Almost 45% of all public schools have reported that they have an SRO assigned to their campuses (Sawchuk, 2019). While most SROs receive training in school shooting prevention, only 54% are trained in interacting with students with disabilities, and fewer than 40% have received training in understanding child trauma (*Education Week,*

2018). The supposed intention for hiring SROs is to increase school safety, but how safe are marginalized students when police are present in school?

If schools are to be safe environments, we must consider that, for example, for many Black youth the police do not represent safety. Police violence in schools, particularly against Black students, is a disturbing and all too common form of trauma. While I was writing this book, a news story from Florida went viral: a six-year-old Black girl was arrested by police in her school. Kaia Rolle, who hadn't slept well the night before, threw a tantrum in her class (developmentally appropriate behavior for her age). School staff attempted to grab her, and when Kaia kicked at them in response, she was arrested (Chiu, 2019). Six years old. Infuriatingly, her story is not unique. Monique W. Morris's book *Pushout: The Criminalization of Black Girls in Schools* (2018) tells the stories of the arrests of six-year-old Desre'e Watson, six-year-old Salecia Johnson, and eight-year-old Jmiyha Rickman, all Black girls who were restrained and arrested by police at schools. Morris notes that "there were others—most of which did not make the nightly news" (p. 57).

Morris explains that Black girls' disproportionate experiences of discipline, suspension, and expulsion stem from adults' biased attitudes toward them. Teachers involve police when they judge that there is a safety issue, and, as Morris wrote, "what constitutes a threat to safety is dangerously subjective when Black children are involved" (p. 57). The confluence of adult bias and racism, zero-tolerance policies for student misbehavior, and police presence can result in real harm, especially to Black students, Indigenous students, and disabled students, all of whom are disproportionately referred to police and arrested in schools (Whitaker et al., 2019). Whether automatic suspension and expulsion due to zero-tolerance policies, or referral to the criminal justice system, the damage is done.

Teachers should be especially concerned with these practices because we are too often complicit in the escalation from challenges in managing classroom behavior to police intervention. This isn't always as simple as teachers literally picking up the phone to call police into the classroom. It can start with small decisions that lead to the criminalization of age-appropriate behavior.

Once while observing in a school I witnessed an interaction between a seemingly distressed teenage girl and her teacher. The student approached her teacher and started to describe how clothes in her gym locker had gone missing and that she felt sure one of her classmates was responsible. The teacher quickly responded that it seemed like a matter for the SRO and encouraged the student to get back to work and check in with the officer later.

While the theft of gym clothes could conceivably be a crime, teenagers messing with one another's belongings is also an age-appropriate conflict, most effectively addressed by teachers, counselors, or school administrators. The redirection of these types of low-level offenses into the juvenile justice system is one way that SROs contribute to the school-to-prison pipeline: the confluence of policies and practices that funnel youth into the juvenile and criminal justice systems. This largely happens through the use of zero-tolerance policies and criminalization of student misconduct, combined with educator bias that leads to harsher discipline of children of color (McNeal, 2016). Some take this concept a step further and conceptualize a "school to prison nexus," in which schools actually operate *as* prisons: "Students are punished if they do not walk on demarcated lines in the floor, are required to remain silent during lunch, required to wear uniforms . . . subject to random searches, and are fined for being out of uniform" (Stovall, 2018, pp. 55–56). These conditions are not trauma-informed; they are trauma-inducing.

Even when students aren't detained or arrested by police, mere interactions with officers can lead to lasting psychological stress. In one study, researchers found that being stopped by the police resulted in emotional distress for youth, including posttraumatic stress symptoms. Even more concerning, the study found that signs of distress were significantly higher when police stops occurred at school compared to any other location (Jackson et al., 2019). How are our trauma-informed approaches considering this kind of trauma?

Any police interaction in schools has to be considered in the context of a country where police violence kills Black people with unacceptable frequency. Police in schools not only are a threat to Black children but also can serve as a constant reminder of this collective trauma.

Curriculum Violence and Racial Trauma. The previous two examples of school-based trauma revolve around peer violence and police violence. The next example may be the most challenging for teachers to grapple with: sometimes teachers cause trauma when we teach.

Curriculum violence is the result of classroom content and pedagogy that harms students intellectually and emotionally. One all-too-common example of curriculum violence: in-class "reenactments" or simulations of historical acts of violence and oppression. Teachers design these activities in the name of "experiential education," but asking students to pretend they are enslaved Africans in the hull of a ship or to walk a simulated Trail of Tears (both, unfortunately, real examples) thrusts students into the painful embodiment of historical trauma. These activities can also have the effect of making light of complex, difficult moments in history, the impacts of which are still felt by communities today.

Jaiden Watson, a Vermont middle school student, experienced curriculum violence when his teacher designed an activity requiring students to pretend to be colonial slave traders. Students traded cards with the word "Negroes" printed on them, along with cards representing guns, tobacco, and cotton. Watson described the experience as making him feel "everything and nothing," both hypervisible in a mostly white school and also diminished to a word on a card (Sabataso, 2020). Experiences of harmful curriculum and instruction often compound students' experiences of racism and harassment by peers within their schools.

While individual teachers are responsible for their equity literacy, the problem of curriculum violence is systemic. Teachers often want their learning to be fun, engaging, and hands on. In a society in which white people are often socialized to believe that it's impolite to talk about race, it's no surprise that white teachers often struggle with effectively teaching about race, issues of identity, and hard histories. My undergraduate teacher preparation program encouraged us to make learning active and hands on and held experiential learning as the gold standard. I don't remember ever discussing the nuance that experiential learning is simply not appropriate when that experience reenacts trauma.

Curriculum violence is just one form of racial trauma in schools. Stephanie P. Jones created the Mapping Racial Trauma in Schools database to track incidents of racism in schools. In looking at hundreds of examples covered in local news media across the country, Jones (2019) identified four main types of school-based racial trauma: (1) curriculum violence from activities that teach difficult histories, such as reenactments of chattel slavery in which students are asked to pretend to be enslavers or enslaved people; (2) digital racial trauma, including images shared through social media, such as a photo of a group of white students in blackface shared online between students; (3) physical violence related to racial trauma; and (4) verbal intimidation and threats between students or from teachers. Jones clarified that, for all of these forms of racial trauma, it doesn't matter whether teachers have good intentions: "Intentionality is not a prerequisite for harmful teaching. Intentionality is also not a prerequisite for racism" (para. 7).

Our Role in the Harm. Bullying and harassment, police presence and violence, and curriculum violence are just three examples of trauma that can occur within the school walls. There are many ways that students can experience harm at school and because of school, and these harms are often compounded when children expect school to be a safe place. All too often students are dismissed and silenced when they try to speak up about the trauma they experience at school, and this dismissal is another form of trauma. Schools commit institutional betrayal when school staff, school culture, or school policies cause trauma, or when they cover it up, fail to respond, or minimize the harm (Smith & Freyd, 2014). This means that schools have multiple layers of responsibility to prevent trauma beyond addressing specific issues like bullying. We also have to understand how our responses and systems can help or harm when students experience trauma at school.

"My mind is popping like movie-theater popcorn," said one of my graduate students after she read a set of articles on how trauma happens within schools. She told me that reading about the concept of curriculum violence brought so many of her past experiences into context. This included situations when she realized she had caused harm but had absolved herself of accountability to her students by clinging to her good intentions. In reflecting on her practice, this teacher recognized that it is our responsibility as the adults in the school to work through the shame and the regret we feel when we harm students so that we can do better in the future.

Let's take this teacher's reflection one step further: as a field, we need to work through the shame and the regret that we have collectively done harm to students. I truly believe in the power of educators to be change makers for social justice. Understanding the harm our students experience in our schools is essential for us to take action to make things better. How have we been complicit in institutional betrayal? Are there times we have been silent for fear of rocking the boat? We need to have hard conversations to uncover all of the ways we as teachers have perpetuated trauma, so that we can see clearly what needs to change.

Now that we've established trauma isn't only something students bring to school from home, and that inequity in our schools causes trauma, let's look at how students may experience school as they deal with the effects of trauma on their lives.

School Isn't Equitable for Trauma-Affected Students

Once students have experienced trauma, how is their access to and experience of their education affected? Based on what we know about how trauma impacts student learning, we can see that school isn't equitable for trauma-affected students. Schools can be indifferent to how trauma affects children, even outright retraumatizing and harmful. If we want school to be equitable for students who have experienced trauma, we need to rethink how common practices in schools are failing our trauma-affected students.

Trauma's Impact on Learning. Imagine you are driving in your car when all of a sudden, a deer leaps out into the road. You slam your foot on the brake pedal and the car stops short. The deer leaps away, and you are unharmed.

How does your body feel in that moment, just after you've slammed on the brakes? Your heart may be racing. You might feel sweaty and flushed. There could be a ringing in your ears, or a general feeling of anxiety and panic. Your stomach might feel like it dropped. In the moment you hit the brakes, you may have shouted out something you otherwise wouldn't say, like swearing at the person sitting next to you. If you have a passenger in the car, you might snap at them even if you weren't in a bad mood beforehand.

These responses all connect to the body's stress-response system. When our brain recognizes that we are in danger, such as being seconds from a car crash, it activates our sympathetic nervous system, which in turn activates our bodies to fight the danger or flee from it (Van der Kolk, 2015). For simplicity's sake, let's call this *survival mode*. Survival mode is something we've all experienced, even if for just that moment after we avoided a car crash.

It typically takes something intense to trigger survival mode, when safety is the default state. Once danger has passed, people with a baseline of safety can return to a feeling of calm and move forward. In contrast, for children who experience trauma, especially chronic trauma, survival mode is activated much more easily. After the stress-response system is activated, they struggle to turn it off if there is no actual danger (Perry & Szalavitz, 2017). Trauma-affected children become finely tuned detectors of their environments. They constantly scan their surroundings for any tiny cue that would help them determine "I am safe" or "I am not safe," even if those cues seem insignificant to others. For example, a student might hear an unexpected banging sound from another classroom. A child who is not in a state of hypervigilance might take a moment to interpret the sound, wonder what's causing it, or simply ignore it. A trauma-affected child's brain says, "Better safe than sorry" and activates the stress-response system.

When a child in the classroom goes into survival mode, the stress response system diverts resources from the parts of the brain and body that do anything other than key survival functions, so complex tasks become out of the question. This doesn't mean that trauma-affected children cannot learn, but children impacted by trauma tend to do worse on markers of academic achievement, such as reading and math scores, and may have challenges with memory, attention, and language skills (Perfect et al., 2016). We should understand this not as evidence that trauma-affected students are poor learners but as evidence that schools need to do more to understand their needs and design instruction that meets those needs while prioritizing a sense of safety.

Yet all too often this doesn't happen. Instead, our choices as educators contribute to our students becoming triggered. Consider the examples of trauma caused within schools from earlier in this chapter. Imagine a student walking between classes who is running late. As he is jogging a little bit to get to class on time, the uniformed school resource officer crosses his path and scolds the student for running in the hallway. The student sees the officer's holstered Taser and hears the harsh tone of his voice, and all of a sudden he is overcome with memories of times when the police have threatened him and his family members in their neighborhood. As the student enters his math class, his brain floods with fear. He feels nauseous and anxious and can barely listen to the instructions being given by his teacher, and he fails the quiz at the end of the period. Is school equitable for this student? Did the leaders of his school set him up for success? How might his teacher have structured the class in ways that helped him regain a sense of safety? How could the student's distress have been prevented in the first place?

Punitive Discipline, Seclusion, and Restraint. Beyond academics, a major barrier for trauma-affected students in school is the response of educators to students in survival mode. Teachers can perpetuate inequity when we choose to see student behavior as defiant or unruly rather than a normal response to stress and trauma. If I don't understand how trauma and survival mode present themselves, I might interpret a student's head being down as disengagement rather than dissociation. I might interpret a student running out of the classroom as disrespectful rather than an effort to keep herself safe through a flight response. I might interpret a student snapping at me as defiance rather than an appropriate response of anger and rage at those who have harmed him or failed to see his pain.

In most schools, this type of behavior elicits a reprimand or consequence from teachers. When we respond in this way, we're punishing students for their survival skills. If trauma-affected students are to equitably access a high-quality education, we cannot punish them for an automatic body-brain response that is trying to keep them safe. A *trauma-indifferent* response to such students treats all unruly behavior as willful defiance or intentional lack of compliance, and teachers apply negative consequences to deter it. A *trauma-inducing* response to such behavior often looks like seclusion and restraint, especially for students identified for individualized education plans (IEPs).

A 2019 Government Accountability Office analysis of seclusion and restraint data (Nowicki, 2019) showed that, while students with disabilities comprised about 12% of the total student population, they accounted for about 76% of students who were physically restrained. Being restrained at school or locked into a seclusion space can be deeply traumatic for students. This type of maltreatment is considered institutional violence, and it happens when adults do things like exploit the power imbalance between disabled students and teachers (Thomas-Skaf & Jenney, 2020).

Seclusion and restraint create an untenable cycle. First, children are triggered by a cue of danger in school. Next, they respond to this danger by going into survival mode, which can sometimes take the form of physical aggression or being "out of control." Teachers and administrators respond to this aggression by physically restraining the children or placing them in a seclusion room, which confirms their feeling that school is not safe. The cycle continues.

Putting our hands on students in any way can cause long-lasting distress. I remember working with one student, Tim, during his sophomore and junior years. Part of my role was to facilitate meetings with Tim and his dad about his progress in school. Tim's attendance was poor, he wasn't engaged in his classes, and he often got into conflicts with his teachers and peers. In our meetings to address these issues, I found that collaborating and building trust were close to impossible. Tim and his dad frequently brought up an incident from Tim's third-grade year. Tim remembered crawling behind a bookshelf when he was upset and then being physically dragged out of his hiding spot by the school's assistant principal. This happened six years before I ever met Tim and in a different school district than the one we were in. Yet Tim was clearly still traumatized by this hands-on altercation with a school leader, and Tim's dad still refused to trust school personnel who might treat his child in a similar way. I don't blame either of them for these responses. The lack of trust was warranted. When we put hands on students in moments of crisis, we may never know how long the impacts will be felt.

When I speak to teachers about the adverse impact of seclusion and restraint, I often hear stories about injuries sustained by teachers during their work with students. I'm not unsympathetic to these teachers, and it is essential that teachers, too, feel safe in the school environment. But seclusion and restraint only perpetuate a lack of safety. Resources and training exist to help schools prevent crises and to use nonpunitive methods of deescalation. Of particular promise: restorative justice, a paradigm shift that focuses on building community and repairing harm between people, rather than compliance and obedience based on rules. Trauma-informed educators have an obligation to make shifts away from punitive discipline so we can end harmful cycles connected to students' survival responses.

Don't Fall Into a Deficit Trap. The previous two examples focus on the challenges for trauma-affected students as they respond to triggers of danger. Even when students aren't actively in survival mode, trauma has been shown to impact other key functions, including sensorimotor development, attention and memory, and executive functioning skills (Craig, 2016). When all of these are combined, students experiencing trauma may face barriers to engaging in their learning if we don't consciously design our classrooms and schools with their needs in mind.

As we acknowledge the truth of these struggles, we also need to be careful how we apply our understanding of survival mode and the potential impacts of trauma on learning. Students who are made to feel unsafe at school are still capable of learning, of building relationships, and of advocating for themselves. We can't view or treat children as though they are permanently damaged by trauma. It can feel like a contradiction to hear "don't ignore the impact of trauma" and also "don't define a child by trauma," but both things can be true at once.

Creating Trauma-Informed Systems, Not Fixing Kids

One of the principles of equity literacy is "fix injustice, not kids" (Gorski, 2019, p. 61). As we seek to address equity issues through our trauma-informed work, we should be aware of how we address the systems that need to change while at the same time we support individual students. Remembering our example of the organic farm, we can't just wash the pesticides off the tomato to make it organic: the soil it grows in needs to change.

As teachers, we are responsible for the kids in front of us, and yet it's not enough to focus only on those students. In her article "Mindfulness Won't Save Us. Fixing the System Will" (2019) middle school teacher Christina Torres wrote about this tension:

> *Teaching students to meditate will help manage their anger or frustration, but it won't remove a system that mass incarcerates their neighbors and family members. Giving students skills in socioemotional learning can help students better process and express their opinions, but it won't erase a system that was built not only to their disadvantage, but also sometimes actively set up to see them fail. Yoga can help a child feel present in their body, but it won't change the fact that our society places different values on different bodies. (para. 5)*

As Torres described, classroom-level social-emotional interventions can provide needed skills and support, but they aren't enough. It can foster a deficit mindset when we look only at how we can help students be more resilient, without considering why they *need* resilience. This mindset says: "If only these kids were more resilient, they wouldn't struggle with trauma so much!" It fools us into thinking that, if students simply had more skills to cope with the pain, that would solve the problem. The thing is, the problem isn't ever the children themselves: the problem is the adults who choose to harm children, or the conditions that adults create that cause harm to children.

This focus on building resilience in individual students is an "equity detour" that allows educators and schools to feel like they are making progress on equity without actually addressing the conditions that cause inequity (Gorski, 2019). Of course, it's wonderful to want to build resilience in students. Resilience against the impacts of trauma is an excellent goal, and all students should have access to strategies that help them bounce back from hard times. I'm not arguing against teaching students social-emotional skills. Instead, I'm advocating that educators hold two approaches at the same time: dismantling unjust systems within and outside of our schools, while also helping students who are currently impacted by these systems. Teaching LGBTQ students to be resilient in the face of homophobic bullying isn't equity— ending homophobia is.

What if, along with teaching mindfulness so that students can cope with the inequitable conditions at school, we help them learn things like grassroots organizing and political advocacy to end those conditions? While mindfulness alone won't fix injustice, it might help trauma-affected students feel emotionally grounded as they step into advocacy work. And while we should support student activism, adults in schools must take the lead in creating equitable conditions. Equity-centered trauma-informed work is about creating resilient schools and systems, not only supporting resilience in individual children.

ACTION STEPS

Becoming fluent in equity literacy can take a lifetime, but there are a wealth of resources to help you on your learning journey. These action steps point you toward some of those resources, as well as some actionable ideas for bringing equity to the center of your practice.

Develop Your Lens

- Develop your equity literacy by visiting the Equity Literacy Institute website (https://www.equityliteracy.org/) for free articles, free online learning, and resources.
- Read more books written by women authors; Black, Indigenous, and people of color authors; Muslim authors; transgender authors; disabled authors. These can be novels, nonfiction, memoirs, or personal essays. Seek out art, movies, and other media from folks with marginalized identities as well. If you are like most Americans, you've been exposed to art and literature created disproportionately by white men, and what stories we do read about marginalized people often focus on their pain or trauma. Reading alone doesn't create equity, but it is an important first step in expand our understanding of the perspectives, inner lives, and strengths of people across identities.

Transform Your Classroom

- Put equity understanding into practice by reflecting on your own classroom through an equity lens and experimenting with your instruction. Cornelius Minor's book *We Got This* (2019) is a great resource, with tools and strategies to go from equity awareness to equity action in your sphere of influence.
- Along with the bigger-picture shifts described in this book, it's also important to address specific learning issues connected to trauma, such as challenges with memory and executive functioning. Collaborate with special educators and occupational therapists in your school to better understand how your instruction can be accessible to all.

Shift the Systems

- Many inequities in school are visible in systems of discipline and response to so-called "challenging" student behavior. Restorative justice practices are one model for moving away from punitive discipline. Learn more about how restorative practices can work for your school, and consider collaborating with a local restorative justice center to begin the work of shifting to more equitable ways of responding to conflict and harm.

- The people with the most accurate information about inequity in your school: your students and community. Expand methods and frequency of gathering student, caregiver, and community feedback about your academic and social-emotional curricula. What do students want to know and be able to do, and what social support and emotional skills do they need help developing? What are their families' and caregivers' hopes and dreams for them? When evaluating your feedback methods, consider multiple methods of connecting and collecting—find a balance between face to face, online, phone, and mail. Provide opportunities for anonymous feedback, as well as relationship-based conversations. Never assume what the community needs: let them tell you in their own words.

Part II

Shift 1: Adopt a Universal Approach

Who needs a trauma-informed environment? When health care providers and researchers originally conceptualized trauma-informed practices, they identified the model as a universal approach. In a 2005 paper on trauma-informed care for women receiving mental health services, a group of practitioners wrote: "Since providers have no way of distinguishing survivors from nonsurvivors, best practices are those that treat all women as if they might be trauma survivors, relying on procedures that are most likely to be growth-promoting and least likely to be retraumatizing" (Elliott et al., 2005, p. 463). Despite the clarity in original definitions of *trauma-informed*, many schools focus on providing support only for students they know to have been impacted by trauma. For example, I've heard teachers say, "If only I knew what was going on at home I would have been more flexible with homework," or "If it's a behavior issue, that's one thing, but if it's trauma, that's another." This creates a false sense that we can increase our flexibility and offer support only if we are privy to details of trauma. If we believe we have to know about the trauma before offering trauma-informed support, then trauma becomes another thing to assess, diagnose, and label.

Trauma is a lens, not a label. This means that trauma should shape how we see school and education. In various ways, trauma impacts us all throughout our lifetime. We may experience it ourselves. We may have loved ones, friends, or family who struggle with trauma. We also live through times of collective grief and trauma in our communities. Attempting to identify which children have experienced trauma and which have not will always be futile: we know that some children can slip under the radar of the adults in their lives, like my mother did. These children suffer in silence. Other children will express their pain through anger and aggression, but we adults will sometimes misinterpret this as defiance or insubordination. When we discipline children who are trying to communicate that they are not okay, we have a tendency to make things worse. Using trauma-informed practices only for certain kids, or just in alternative classrooms, misses the mark and leaves kids behind.

As I was completing the manuscript for this book in the spring of 2020, the coronavirus pandemic shut down public schools around the world. Teachers, parents, and education leaders scrambled to figure out how to deliver academic instruction from a distance, trying to maintain relationships between school and students while also attending to massive equity issues like internet access and food insecurity. I'm friends with a small group of educators who also work on trauma-informed practices and equity. We all experienced a sudden surge of interest in our work. We heard from teachers and schools across the country that they needed to better understand trauma, given the pandemic. In discussing this, my colleagues and I agreed that we were grateful for the interest, but also saddened: why did it take a global crisis for so many to see that trauma impacts us all?

Not long after the pandemic landed in the United States, police officers in Minneapolis killed George Floyd, sparking a global protest movement to reaffirm that Black lives matter. My friend shea martin (2020), an educator and antiracist teaching advocate, tweeted: "What a time to be alive and be an antiracist consultant. i wonder if this is how kale felt after Beyoncé wore that sweatshirt." Although the tweet made light of the surge of public attention, shea also shared the feeling I had a few weeks earlier: why did it take *this* to capture the public's attention? Racism has been part of the United States since the country came to exist and has always been present in our education system. While the increase in awareness of both trauma-informed and equity-centered practices is good news overall, it highlights a problem: these practices should have already been a priority.

We need a shift. We can no longer be reactive. We can't wait until after a racist incident to address racism. We can't wait until after an individual or community crisis to address trauma. Part II explores the first of the four shifts: *Shift from a reactive stance, in which we identify who has been traumatized and support them, to a proactive approach. Trauma-informed practices are universal and benefit everyone.* A proactive, universal approach not only helps individual students impacted by trauma but also creates a more equitable and trauma-informed environment for everyone in the school community.

This shift is necessary to move us closer to these principles of equity-centered trauma-informed education:

- **Principle 2: Asset based**—Trauma-informed education is asset based and doesn't attempt to fix kids, because kids are not broken. Instead, it addresses the conditions, systems, and structures that harm kids.
- **Principle 4: Human centered**—Trauma-informed education means centering our shared humanity.
- **Principle 5: Universal and proactive**—Trauma-informed education is a universal approach, implemented proactively.

The following chapters explore some of the ways that schools can begin to implement trauma-informed practices as they were originally intended: as a paradigm shift, not as an add-on. Using the lens of wellness, we will consider how schools can proactively create environments that respond to and prevent trauma (Chapter 4), and four proactive priorities that help us make decisions about classroom and school practices (Chapter 5). First, Chapter 3 begins with a conversation about the adverse childhood experiences score.

3 | Trauma Is More Than a Number

To understand why we need to shift to a universal approach, we have to examine what we're shifting from. Labeling and sorting students based on their experiences of trauma is harmful, but this has become common practice in formal and informal ways. One of the main culprits of this labeling: the adverse childhood experience (ACE) score.

While attending a large education conference, I participated in a breakout group of teachers to discuss a shared interest in trauma-informed education. We sat in a circle and shared some of the resources and strategies we were using in our schools. Many teachers referred to the ACEs, introduced by a landmark study that linked childhood trauma to negative health outcomes throughout a person's life (Felitti et al., 1998). The ACE Study is cited often by educators because its findings validate what so many of us have observed in our own students over the years: trauma has long-lasting and powerful impacts on the minds and bodies of children, long after the traumatic event has ended.

Vincent Felitti and Robert Anda conducted the ACE Study in partnership with Kaiser Permanente and the Centers for Disease Control and Prevention. Based on a survey of over 17,000 California residents, the study found that there was a strong correlation between adverse experiences in childhood, such as physical abuse, and negative health outcomes later in life. For example, individuals who reported experiencing four or more ACEs were almost twice as likely to develop cancer than those who reported none, and almost four times as likely to develop chronic bronchitis or emphysema (Felitti et al., 1998).

Before the ACE Study, the prevailing view about trauma was that it was mainly an emotional problem. Felitti and Anda's research shifted the conversation, moving childhood trauma into the sphere of public health. There are now numerous studies examining the long-range impacts of ACEs, such as the risk for specific diseases, the likelihood of opioid abuse, and employment success, just to name a few. ACE research has been used as the foundation for changes in state and federal education law, with bills citing the study as evidence of the need for trauma-informed policy. In education, advocates of trauma-informed practices often invoke ACEs as evidence of the need for a trauma-informed approach. Indeed, this book joins almost every single other book on trauma-informed education to cite this specific study (see Craig, 2016; Sporleder & Forbes, 2016; Souers & Hall, 2016; Jennings, 2019).

Back in the conference breakout room, a young teacher sitting across from me spoke about her new charter school, where the administration really wanted to weave trauma-informed practices into the fabric of the school. "It starts out really simple, actually," she shared. "We just do the ACE checklist during school intake. That way we know each student's ACE score."

Record scratch. Hearing this shocked me, and sadly, it wouldn't be the last time I heard about a school using a similar strategy—far from it, in fact. You see, the ACE "checklist" that this teacher mentioned is a problematic off-shoot of the ACE Study. When Felitti and Anda designed the survey for their research, they identified a handful of adverse experiences about which to ask their participants. They asked participants about whether they had experienced physical or sexual abuse, whether any household members had problems with substance abuse or mental illness, and whether they had witnessed their mothers being treated violently, for example, along with a few other questions about abuse and dysfunction in the household. The number of items that a participant said they had experienced became an "ACE score," which was then used in the study to demonstrate correlations between the number of adverse experiences and health outcomes.

The concept of an ACE score captured the interest of the public. Soon, the questions from the original study were turned into a simple checklist that anyone can fill out to find their personal ACE score. You can easily find an ACE checklist online, and versions of ACE checklists are reprinted in many books about trauma and trauma-informed education. I'm not reprinting one here, for reasons that will soon be clear.

So, why did the teacher I met at the conference want to find an ACE score for the students in her school? She told me that she wanted to identify which students were in need of support, and her thinking was that the ACE score would provide a simple way to accomplish this. The ACE scores would also give the school some data on the overall level of trauma among the student body. Since meeting that teacher, I've heard the same reasoning from many other educators and school administrators who use the ACE checklist as a screening tool with their students. I understand the good intentions behind this idea, but it can have negative unintended consequences for students. I'll share with you what I shared with the teacher at the conference: using ACE scores in schools is a harmful practice. Child trauma is far more than a number.

In an equity-centered trauma-informed school, we should never administer the ACE checklist and never ask students or faculty to share an ACE score. Doing so can retraumatize students rather than help them. The ACE score also has the potential to become a label that stigmatizes students. At the same time, the ACE checklist is incomplete and doesn't actually tell us much about how to help trauma-affected kids. Robert Anda, the co-investigator of the ACE Study, was the lead author on a 2020 paper discouraging the use of the ACE checklist as an individual inventory. Concerned with the way that the ACE checklist has been used since the original study, he wrote, "The ACE score is not a standardized measure of childhood exposure to the biology of stress" (Anda et al., 2020, p. 1).

Because the ACE checklist appears in so many trauma-informed education resources, let's dig a little deeper into its potential harms so we can understand what to do instead.

The Trouble With ACEs

Picture this: You are swimming in the ocean, a little way out from the shore. You are surprised when a wave suddenly breaks where you are standing, and you are pulled underwater. The experience is overwhelming and stressful. But not all stress becomes trauma. There are many factors that shape whether a stressful event is traumatizing, including context, past experiences, and community support. A pro surfer, for example, might regularly contend with big waves and therefore has the skills and experience she needs to safely navigate the water. A three-year-old child on his first visit to the beach may be terrified and may experience flashbacks and fear when he goes to the beach for years to come. Trauma is in our experience of and response to the wave, not the wave itself.

Because trauma is subjective, the ACE checklist doesn't provide a meaningful understanding of a person's experience with trauma. The checklist asks, did you experience these events, yes or no? The higher the score, the more types of adversity a person has experienced. But the number is misleading. A child who experienced sexual abuse, had an incarcerated father, and whose parents got divorced would have an ACE score of 3. The number 3 hides important information: was the sexual abuse prolonged or did it happen once? Was the divorce stressful and contentious, or did it actually create a more peaceful home? Who supported the family when the child's father went to prison? Furthermore, the ACE checklist focuses only on adversity that happens in the home. As discussed in Chapter 2, trauma doesn't happen only at home. If a student developed trauma from incessant bullying in his third-grade classroom, that trauma goes unaccounted for in an ACE checklist. Felitti and Anda's study demonstrated the impact of childhood adversity on the broader population, but it doesn't tell us anything about the personal experience behind the numbers. For teachers, knowing that your students have an ACE score of 1 or 8 won't help you understand how those experiences impact them. Knowing a student's "score" may give you a false sense of your students' lived experiences.

How we experience trauma is complicated. A trauma response is shaped by how we respond to threat, our networks of support and access to resources, and our personal and cultural histories of trauma. The way we think about trauma needs to be nuanced. For teachers, this means not making assumptions about how our students experience stressful events or conditions. For example, students who live in poverty aren't automatically traumatized. The simplicity of the ACE score makes it tempting to use: couldn't it help streamline how we offer supports and services? Unfortunately, there is no way to simplify trauma.

ACE Checklists in Action

There are additional problems with using ACE checklists in schools, beyond the limited information we get. First, mental health and trauma screening in school is a complex issue. While it may seem simple to run through a checklist of yes/no questions, therapeutic screening requires skills and expertise. Clinicians need to choose research-validated tools (which the ACE checklist is not), consider legal and ethical issues such as parental and child consent, and understand the difference between screening and diagnosis. Because of the complexities involved and limited evidence that it's even effective, trauma screening in schools, even when administered by clinicians, is generally not recommended (Eklund et al., 2018). Needless to say, if schools do decide to administer trauma screening, it should never be facilitated by teachers or other nonclinical staff.

What about using the ACE checklist as an informational or educational tool? High school teachers or college instructors are sometimes interested in teaching students about trauma, and the ACE checklist can appear to be an easy-to-understand teaching tool. Many teachers see an example of this in the popular documentary *Paper Tigers* (2015), which chronicles an alternative high school in Washington state that implements trauma-informed practices. In the opening moments of *Paper Tigers*, a classroom teacher asks students to report their ACE score anonymously, using clickers. The students' scores are then displayed in a graph on the projector screen. One student becomes visibly agitated in the follow-up discussion, upset by the teacher's assertion that parents pass unresolved trauma to their children. The bell rings and cuts off the discussion, leaving the students to make sense of this information on their own.

Imagine the experience of that student. In your class, you learn that trauma can have lifelong impacts on health and wellness. Sitting in a room among your friends and classmates, you look at a list of items: sexual abuse, neglect, substance abuse, divorce. You check "yes" next to some of these items. You feel your heart beating fast and your face flushes as memories flash through your mind, memories that tell the story behind each "yes" answer. You punch the number 4 into your clicker and watch as the graph on the projector screen populates. You see that about half of your peers have scores of eight, nine, or ten. With a sinking feeling in your stomach, you wonder whether what happened to you was all that bad, given that others in your class have it worse. Your teacher ends class quickly and you walk in a fog to your next class, overwhelmed with anxiety and left with too many questions. You don't trust the school counselor and you can't afford therapy, so you will have to make sense of your newly named trauma on your own. Does this activity help promote equity within the school? Is this activity trauma-informed? Or is it likely to make school a less safe and more challenging learning environment?

Some of us may not have to imagine this scenario because we have experienced it in professional development. When I talk to groups of teachers about the harms of ACE checklists, there are always a few who say they have been asked to find their own ACE score in a professional development session at their school. Reflecting on our own experiences can be helpful to our teaching practice, but teachers should never be required to sit among coworkers and reflect on traumatic childhood memories.

From a Checklist to a Universal Approach

It may seem paradoxical to say that in a trauma-informed school we don't need to know who has experienced trauma. It is a paradigm shift: rather than a medical model where people get help only after a diagnosis, trauma-informed practices are preventative and holistic. One of the goals of trauma-informed practices is to decrease stigma about trauma.

When we use ACE scores, we work against that goal. As Alex Winninghoff (2020) explained in her article "Trauma by Numbers,"

> *It is often claimed that the trauma-informed movement should move school discipline away from a message to students that "there is something wrong with them" to a message that "something happened to them." But the underlying logic and practices of the ACE frameworks and scores contribute to a continuation of social narratives that tell students there is something wrong with them* because *something happened to them. (p. 40; emphasis added)*

When we use simplistic definitions of trauma or try to label and sort our students into "traumatized" and "not traumatized" categories, we send the message that trauma makes you different. This can also have the effect of creating a division between students and teachers, with students as the ones in need of help and teachers as nontraumatized helpers (Dutro, 2017). The truth is that trauma is a part of the human experience, so everyone in the school community may need a trauma-informed environment. Everyone benefits from the universal application of trauma-informed practices.

ACTION STEPS

Just as medical professionals take an oath to do no harm to their patients, so should teachers vow to end harmful practices like ACE checklists. These action steps suggest some steps for ending harm and expanding our perspective.

Develop Your Lens

- Many educators were introduced to trauma-informed education using the ACE checklist. If you're one of them, it's important to expand your understanding of trauma so you don't get stuck in an ACE mindset. For a deep dive, read *Trauma and Recovery* (1992/2015) by Judith Herman. For shorter resources, explore the National Child Traumatic Stress Network website (NCTSN.org), which has resources on different types of trauma, including historical trauma, community trauma, and traumatic grief, along with free webinars and online classes.

Transform Your Classroom

- One of the lessons that I take away from the ACE controversy is that just because something is simple and popular does not make it true. Understanding trauma requires our critical thinking and ability to explore contradictory ideas. These are skills that serve us well in so many areas of life. How might you help students develop their own critical thinking so they can recognize similar issues in their areas of interest or professional fields?

Shift the Systems

- If your school is one that uses any version of the ACE checklist for student screening, end that practice as soon as possible. Encourage school mental health staff (counselors, psychologists, or social workers) to engage with their professional associations and current research to make informed decisions about trauma screening in school.

4 | Trauma Is a Lens, Not a Label

Equity-centered trauma-informed practices should be both proactive and universal. I use the word *universal* here to draw a connection between these practices and universal design for learning (UDL). UDL is an approach to accessibility that evolved from the architectural practice of universal design, in which accessibility features (e.g., ramps) are built in proactively and can be used by anyone, rather than adding in options for accessibility as an afterthought. UDL follows the same principle of proactive accessibility features in learning environments that are available to everyone, rather than responsively provided only to certain students.

Trauma-informed practices aren't just about decreasing problem behavior or restoring order after a crisis. Equity work isn't just about fixing racial disparities in test scores. Both trauma-informed work and equity-centered work are part of a universal drive toward justice in which an affirming, invigorating educational experience is a right for every student. So, equity-centered trauma-informed work needs to follow a universal approach that touches every part of a school community in proactive ways.

How Is Trauma Present in Our School?

An individual approach to trauma asks, When students are impacted by trauma, how should we respond? It's an essential question to ask, but it's incomplete. By focusing only on individuals, we miss how trauma can impact the entire school environment. For example, if there is one student in a class of 25 who is going through a crisis, the school might respond one way. If 20 out of the 25 students are in crisis simultaneously, that requires a different response. An entire class in crisis might mean that there is something traumatic about the school environment. We need to see the big picture. Individual interventions won't do anything to solve a community-wide problem.

A starting place for educators in creating a universal approach to equity-centered trauma-informed practices is to ask, How is trauma present in our school? This question is inspired by Paul Gorski, who asks schools to consider, How does racism operate in our school? (His question will help you answer mine, by the way). Asking how trauma is present in schools shifts the focus away from examining the behavior of individual students and instead focuses on how trauma affects the entire school community. Here are some additional questions to help you answer the overarching one:

- How does trauma in our society impact our school?
- How does historical and community trauma impact our town? Our neighborhood? Our school?
- How does trauma impact our teachers? Our leaders? Our students?
- How does trauma impact the families and caregivers of our students?
- What are the healing practices of our community?
- What are the coping strategies used by students? By teachers? By families and caregivers? By leaders?
- How is trauma created in our school?
- How is trauma healed in our school?

What other questions can you ask about how trauma is present in your school? Begin these discussions with your colleagues. To be trauma-informed we need to first learn to recognize it and understand it in our settings.

If we can't see trauma, we can struggle to change our teaching practice. For example, it's common for teachers to start the school year with some type of writing prompt or project to answer the question, "What did you do this summer?" If I'm a teacher who typically enjoys summer as a time to take off from work, spend time outdoors, and catch up with friends, this might seem like a reasonable question to ask. But we know that not all people experience summer as a positive time. Being out of school can mean increased food insecurity for families, isolation and loneliness for some students, or long hours of work. For other students, summer means international travel, camps, or increased independence. If we ask, How is trauma present?, we can see that some students may have experienced traumatic conditions and events over the summer. Some students may experience anxiety or fear returning to school because school is a harmful place. Students may be worried that they will be judged or bullied by peers based on how they answer, "What did you do this summer?" This doesn't mean we never ask students about their lives, but it does mean that we do so with a full understanding of how students may experience such questions.

Asking how trauma operates in your school can also bring your attention to the bigger picture. Some communities have historical trauma directly connected to school itself. For example, Indigenous children in the Americas were forced to attend residential schools, with the goal of assimilating these children into white culture. The schools cut students' hair, punished them for speaking their native languages, and in many cases abused them. This horror of the residential school experience is one facet of historical trauma for Indigenous peoples (Bombay et al., 2014; Pember, 2019). For families impacted by this historical trauma, schools may still represent a place of forced assimilation and erasure. We should learn about this type of historical trauma narrative to fully understand how trauma is present in our education system. If we don't, we risk ignoring the essential context that sets the stage for everything that happens in our schools.

A universal equity-centered trauma-informed approach requires that we are intentional in creating safety and trust. But trust and safety aren't established just because we say, "You can trust me," or "This is a safe space." Noticing and naming how trauma operates in our school and community can help us consider what it will take to create safe and affirming environments. School is not a blank slate or a fresh start each fall. Critical disability studies scholar Irene H. Yoon wrote that schools are "haunted" by the ghosts of injustices they have committed as institutions: "Ghosts demand justice, which is why they haunt" (2019, p. 424). We must face these ghosts as we seek to create social justice in our schools.

Fostering Critical Wellness

The heart of a universal equity-centered trauma-informed approach is a focus on each school community member as a whole person. As I stated in Table 1.1, in describing Principle 4 of equity-centered trauma-informed education—*trauma-informed education means centering our shared humanity*—dehumanization causes trauma, and equity cannot exist in schools that dehumanize students or staff. Humanizing school requires that we dispense with the outdated idea that children or adults can somehow divorce their brains from their bodies. Why do schools so often pretend that it's possible to leave our emotional and physical selves outside of school and bring only our intellectual selves into the classroom? This expectation runs against all available learning science and psychology. Schools need to change so that children and adults can bring their whole selves with them. What is more, schools need to be places that increase our personal and community wellness, not deplete it.

What does it mean to be well? In the most basic sense, I see wellness as the condition in which our basic needs are met, including eating, sleeping, movement, safety, and emotional connection. Wellness is sometimes considered an individual pursuit, but in a trauma-informed environment we should consider wellness a community effort. In the book *All Students Must Thrive* (2019), Tyrone C. Howard and other contributors define the term *critical wellness* as encompassing wellness, critical pedagogy, and critical race theory. Howard recommended that educators "develop a healthy understanding of historical, political and economic structures that have a profound impact on students' ability to learn. To do anything less is professionally irresponsible and unfair to students and disrupts efforts for optimal student wellness" (p. 5). The understanding of *structures* helps us see how wellness cannot be a solo endeavor. For example, a transgender teen can work to cultivate his own wellness, but as of this writing, it is legal for doctors to refuse to provide health care for him. At many schools, trans youth are not allowed to access single-stall bathrooms and face harassment for using gendered restrooms. These social and political factors impede these students' wellness. When we as educators understand these structures, we can help our students navigate them, and we can work to dismantle them.

The idea of critical wellness captures an essential idea for equity-centered trauma-informed educators. It's impossible to encourage individuals to foster wellness if we ignore the structures and historical context that impact each of us and our capacity to be well. Bettina Love highlights this context in her book *We Want to Do More Than Survive* (2019), explaining that the education system replicates the racism and inequities of our larger society, creating an "educational survival complex" for Black, Indigenous, and other children of color, who are often forced to simply survive the harsh conditions of schools, and this focus on survival limits their ability to truly thrive and be well. Love goes on to make the case for teachers to be abolitionists of the educational survival complex. Being well is central to being an abolitionist educator: "Wellness is a part of social justice work. There must be an inner life that refuses to be less than human" (p. 156).

In many schools, teachers and students alike are dehumanized. Teachers are subject to dehumanizing working conditions. The fact that teachers' schedules often do not allow adequate time for bathroom breaks during the school day has become a joke, but it's just about the least funny thing I can imagine. At the most basic level, treating one another like humans means creating spaces where we can meet our body's needs. It can feel overwhelming to consider how to foster critical wellness when the working conditions of many teachers deny us our most basic needs. I talk more about teacher wellness in Chapter 9, where I speak directly to administrators about fostering critical wellness in their teaching staff.

As teachers, we sometimes then pass the dehumanization we feel along to our students by attempting to control their bodies, too, such as limiting their bathroom access, requiring students to sit a certain way, disciplining them if they do not walk in straight lines. Many schools attempt wellness initiatives through offering group exercise opportunities, providing students with reusable water bottles, or stocking healthier snacks in vending machines. While those may be helpful, a real wellness initiative needs to begin with recognizing our shared humanity. Real wellness can't happen if we attempt to control one another's bodies. Trauma often involves the restriction of our movement or attacks on our body without our consent. When schools replicate that same dynamic, we retraumatize students. Wellness begins by ending that harm.

Universal equity-centered trauma-informed practices should help lift up all members of a school community so that we all have the opportunity to feel safe, to thrive, and to grow. It is not up to teachers or students to just self-care their way into a state of perfect mental health and wellness. Instead, we need a focus on our shared humanity to drive school-wide and system-wide change.

Universal Is Not One-Size-Fits-All

One of the common universal approaches recommended for trauma informed schools is social-emotional learning (SEL). But is SEL really trauma informed? Not always. We should practice using our equity literacy and trauma-informed lens to question whether SEL helps or harms.

SEL is an intentional focus on the development of social and emotional skills and competencies in schools, for both teachers and students. The Coalition for Academic, Social, and Emotional Learning (CASEL) highlights five core competencies for SEL focus: self-awareness, self-management, social awareness, relationship skills, and responsible decision making (CASEL, n.d.). Schools take a variety of approaches to SEL. Some use prepackaged lessons that can be implemented by classroom teachers during class time or during advisory meetings. Other schools focus on a school-wide theme or encourage teachers to integrate social-emotional vocabulary into their everyday practice.

On the surface, SEL is a powerful idea. It calls for the integration of our social and emotional selves along with the academic and intellectual tasks of school. SEL can be an equity tool for trauma-affected students who need more intentional practice and support with social skills and emotional management. But on its own SEL doesn't actually address trauma, racism, or inequity. In fact, implementing SEL can perpetuate traumatic environments if we focus too much on giving students the tools to manage their traumatic stress rather than addressing the causes of that stress. SEL can be weaponized if schools emphasize self-regulation and "calming down" as core skills rather than affirming that there are times to harness righteous anger (Communities for Just Schools Fund, 2020). Dena Simmons, assistant director at the Yale Center for Emotional Intelligence, is both an advocate of and vocal critic of SEL. Simmons has said that, if we teach things like conflict resolution but not "the conflicts that exist because of racism or white supremacy," then SEL can become "white supremacy with a hug" (quoted in Madda, 2019).

Although the CASEL competencies are by far the more prevalent in discussions of SEL, they are not the only way to think about an SEL framework. Teacher educator Patrick Carmangian offers a way of thinking about SEL that is grounded in humanization, saying that teachers "must engage students in ways that help them more effectively manage fear, anxiety, grief, powerlessness, and other various forms of social toxicity that come as a result of structural violence" (Howard, 2019, p. 126). In Carmangian's vision of SEL, the core competencies for students are knowledge of self, solidarity, and self-determination.

To practice using your equity-centered trauma-informed lens, consider the following questions:

- Compare the five CASEL competencies (self-awareness, self-management, social awareness, relationship skills, and responsible decision-making) with Carmangian's three concepts (knowledge of self, solidarity, self-determination). What do you notice? What do you wonder?
- How did you respond to Simmons's description of decontextualized SEL as "white supremacy with a hug"? What are the harms of SEL as it's currently implemented in many schools?
- What social and emotional competencies are needed by antiracists? What are the competencies that help advocates and activists? What competencies help disrupt the causes of trauma?

Universal is not the same thing as one-size-fits-all. To implement powerful SEL, we need to have a deep understanding of our students, our community, and ourselves. We need to make visible the belief systems that can be hidden in supposedly "neutral" frameworks like the CASEL competencies.

Instead, a universal approach means that we focus on humanizing school for all students. We provide flexibility for all students, regardless of whether we know they need it or not. We make mental health support barrier-free and invite all students to take part, whether or not they've been formally identified. All of the trauma-informed practices described in this book can benefit all students. Chapter 5 further discusses some of the proactive approaches we can take to create universal equity-centered trauma-informed schools.

Responsive Supports for All

We should also consider how our responsive supports—that is, the services or interventions we offer to students already impacted by trauma—can be universal and barrier-free. Proactive approaches work best when paired with a robust and flexible set of responsive approaches. Even in the most proactive environment, sometimes people need additional help with their wellness and mental health. Part of a universal approach should be to make additional support accessible to anyone who needs it, with as few barriers as possible. These supports are not just about trauma but about mental health and wellness more broadly.

Trauma is one reason that students or staff might struggle with mental and emotional health, but it's not the only one. About 16% of children have a mental health disorder, and almost half of those children do not receive the treatment or counseling they need (Whitney & Peterson, 2019). More than 4 million children—or a little more than 1 in 20—lack health insurance (Berchick & Mykyta, 2019). Schools alone are not responsible for addressing this great need, but we must do our part.

Many schools organize their social-emotional supports through a multitiered system of support (MTSS) structure. Within an MTSS approach, schools frequently implement positive behavioral interventions and supports (PBIS), a behaviorist framework focused on teaching behavioral expectations and rewarding students who demonstrate compliance with these expectations. The PBIS/MTSS model focuses on universal support to encourage good behavior, with additional interventions for students with problem behaviors.

In a typical MTSS structure, there are three tiers: tier 1 is universal support available to all students, tier 2 involves small-group interventions for some, and tier 3 comprises individualized interventions for just a few identified students. In resources on trauma-informed practices, many experts recommend using this tiered structure (Stratford et al., 2020). For example, a tier 1 practice might be to teach mindfulness strategies to all and implement a school-wide token economy to reward students for following expectations. A common tier 2 intervention is check-in, check-out, a system for students to connect with the same teacher twice each day to work on behavioral goals. A tier 3 intervention is typically more intensive, such as wraparound service coordinated with community health agencies (Jennings, 2019).

Though it may be tempting to simply plug trauma-informed and equity-centered practices into an MTSS model, we should think critically about combining these approaches. Because PBIS and MTSS are based on behavior modification (Knestrict, 2019), they are fundamentally incompatible with trauma-informed practices. In equity-centered trauma-informed practice, the focus is on humanization, critical wellness, and community. Behavior modification, even when wrapped up in cute point systems and feel-good assemblies, is designed to enforce compliance (usually to white-centric, heteropatriarchal norms). Children affected by trauma need an environment that is based on consent, not coercion. Behavior modification is not trauma-informed, which means that PBIS, while often recommended in trauma-informed education resources, is not a trauma-informed approach.

Beyond the behaviorist roots of PBIS, we should be wary of the ever-present MTSS "pyramid" and its tiers. Whether a child "needs" a higher-tier intervention is typically based on the child's adherence to school-created norms that place high value on order and compliance (Bornstein, 2017). Thus, MTSS tiers too often become euphemisms, with teachers using the tiers as coded language for children who do not fit into narrow definitions of "appropriate behavior." "Tier 3 student" isn't a label we should apply to any child, just as we shouldn't apply the label "trauma kid."

MTSS tiers can also give the false sense that a certain type of student needs extra support, as schools tend to identify noncompliant students for higher-level interventions. In reality, we all need extra support sometimes, and that has nothing to do with who we are as people or how well we follow rules. For example, if a student's sibling unexpectedly dies, she may need intensive support for a brief period of time. Intensive support is usually categorized as tier 3, but an otherwise compliant student who needs some extra help may simply receive grace and flexibility from her teachers, while a disruptive student may be pathologized through a tier 3 label, marking her as lacking social-emotional skills. I encourage schools to critically examine which students are identified for which tiers and to disaggregate this data by race, gender, and free and reduced lunch status. What do you notice about the patterns? You may find similar results as research demonstrating that boys and students of color, particularly African American students, are disproportionately identified for higher-tier intervention (Reno et al., 2017). This disproportionality is due to white social norms about what it means to "behave" and who gets punished the most when they do not conform.

Instead of slotting trauma-informed practices into existing MTSS pyramids, schools might consider instead asking these questions:

- What resources, strategies, or approaches for promoting mental health and critical wellness are available to the whole school community?
- How might we be more transparent about the resources available to students?
- How can we increase awareness of the resources available?
- How can we decrease stigma around accessing these resources?
- What is our process for identifying students who need more support? What are our indicators?
- What is our process for collaborating with students and their caregivers when identifying possible resources or supports to try?

- How do we know if our support is helping? What indicators might we use other than tracking misbehavior?

By moving beyond MTSS tiers and PBIS points, we can create a more nuanced and connected system of support for all students.

Support for Students Who Will Never Ask

Being proactive with our trauma-informed practices won't fix all of the challenges our schools face. So much is out of our control, and traumatic events and conditions persist while we work to end them. Some children (and adults) in our schools will need individualized, trauma-specific interventions and support. Yet focusing on what we can do proactively helps reduce the need for the pathologizing or labeling individuals.

In an essay for the magazine *Educational Leadership*, Dena Simmons wrote about how her high achievement in school masked the trauma she was experiencing:

> *The fact is that while many people exhibit typical signs of trauma, many others, like me, have found ways to cope by pouring themselves into work to avoid the discomfort of their distress. Too often, the trauma of high achievers, especially those of color, goes unrecognized because their achievements are sometimes mistaken for resilience. While some of us may be excelling thanks to having a caring adult and other supports in our lives, the scars of our past remain, and we are still in need of care, love, and healing. (2020, para. 6)*

Simmons's story reminds me of the story of my mother that I shared in the introduction. A student like Simmons or my mom may never reach out for help while in school and may never be identified for mental health interventions and services. For every person brave enough to share a story of personal trauma, there are hundreds who never will. We can't wait for more evidence to justify the need for universal trauma-informed and mental health supports in schools. It's time to take action.

ACTION STEPS

Thinking critically about our current school environments is an important first step. Then, we can look to implement proactive and responsive universal strategies to foster critical wellness. Here are some potential steps to take as you build your universal approach:

Develop Your Lens

- To learn more about bringing humanization to the center of education, read Bettina Love's book *We Want to Do More Than Survive* (2019). Her work has essential messages for educators on wellness, survival, and what it means to teach for social justice.
- Use the questions from this chapter to answer the question, How does trauma operate in our school and our community? This can make a powerful individual exercise or a community conversation among your coworkers.

Transform Your Classroom

- Work to destigmatize conversations about mental health in your classroom, especially around getting help. Talk regularly about ways to get help when you're having a hard time. Invite school counselors or social workers to join your class for community building so that students have real relationships with these support people.

Shift the Systems

- Learn about school-based health models and consider whether any elements of school-based health services would work for your community. School-based health services help remove access barriers for students and families, which promotes community wellness. The School-Based Health Alliance (https://www.sbh4all .org/) is a source for more information.

5 | Four Proactive Priorities for Decision Making

How many decisions do teachers make in a day? Sometimes when I'm teaching, I imagine steam coming out of my ears like a cartoon as my mind goes into overdrive making decisions: Where should I stand to capture the class's attention? How loud should I speak so I can be heard but not overwhelming? What tone of voice will communicate how seriously I want students to take my feedback? Should I start with a reading or with a pair activity? Should I create groups or let students self-select? How many minutes can I spend on this topic before we need to move on? Should I address those students whispering or let it go? The list of decisions goes on and on, and those are just ones I make during my actual class. Thousands more I consider while planning, creating curriculum, and designing learning activities.

For equity-centered trauma-informed practices to be a universal approach, we need to infuse trauma and equity awareness into our decision making. This is perhaps the most literal sense of being trauma-informed: when our thought process is *informed* by trauma. To make things easier for myself when I'm planning and making decisions, I boiled down much of what I've learned about trauma into four priorities:

- Predictability
- Flexibility

- Empowerment
- Connection

Each of those priorities is based on a key theme of understanding about how trauma impacts children and their learning. If I prioritize these four areas, I'm infusing my trauma awareness into my planning. Focusing on these priorities can help make learning more equitable for trauma-affected students, but it's also good practice for all students.

These priorities aren't in any particular order of importance or emphasis. The idea is that together they serve as guideposts that help us make decisions about how we do school. If you are a classroom teacher, you may read some of the suggestions in this section and think to yourself, "That would be nice for my students, but I'm not treated that way by my administrators." This is an important point—teachers need these same four priorities in their working conditions to fully realize them for their students. In Chapter 9 I speak directly to school leaders about creating trauma-informed environments for their teachers.

Empowerment

Many people affected by trauma experience a profound sense of powerlessness (Herman, 1992/2015). Trauma most often results from events and circumstances outside of a child's control, whether an adult abusing a position of authority or a natural disaster outside of human influence. This is then compounded when institutions and the people within them replicate unhealthy power dynamics. This can happen when children disclose abuse and then are made to talk to law enforcement officers or engage in counseling with no ability to opt out. For children struggling to feel any sense of control over their own lives, school can be just another place where they are made to comply and punished when they don't.

For children of color, LGBTQ youth, and children in other marginalized communities, this powerlessness is magnified. Youth have their own power but are pushed to the margins and kept from using that power through oppressive policies and attitudes. There is a long-standing dynamic in America, rooted in white supremacy, of white people exerting control over the bodies of people of color. This control isn't just in the past with the enslavement of African people and Jim Crow laws. In the present day there are still rules on the books in schools banning hairstyles that are most commonly worn by African Americans, such as a school in Texas that suspended senior DeAndre Arnold in 2020 for refusing to cut his hair, styled in dreadlocks (Beachum, 2020). Such policies are racist, no matter the supposed intent or "color neutral" enforcement behind them. Controlling the bodies of our students, especially our students of color, is trauma inducing, not trauma-informed.

Yet teachers get messages all the time about controlling our students and their bodies, sometimes literally hearing the message to "control your classroom." Just as we can't foster wellness if we are controlling student bodies, we also can't build empowerment if we are using power over students. It's beyond time to resist and end these types of controlling practices in schools.

To be trauma-informed and equity-centered, we need to prioritize the empowerment and agency of each person in our school communities. By *empowerment* I don't mean simply feeling good about oneself. Rather, true empowerment is claiming and using one's own power. Fostering empowerment starts at a very basic level with ceasing all attempts to control people's bodies within schools. Teachers and students need to be free to use bathrooms when they need to, sit how they want to, and move in whatever way works for them. We also need to revise dress codes and other restrictive policies. Enforcement of strict dress codes puts teachers in a position of policing students' bodies, which negates the rest of the learning relationship.

Flattening the imbalance of power also means reexamining our curricular choices. Students' lives are full of rich areas for exploration and real problems to solve. We don't need to give students fake work that is meaningless in the context of their lives. If we want to help students recognize and use their own power in the world, we need to make sure that our academics are aligned with that goal. I explore this idea more in Part V, which discusses how our curriculum can be a force for justice.

Finally, empowerment means that, when we consider student

support for mental health or behavioral challenges, students *must* be partners in decision making in their own access to and use of services. In too many schools, discussions about how to help students can go pretty far before we actually ask students and their families what they want and need. At the therapeutic school where I taught, the clinical director would remind counseling staff that their role was to be a "counsel to the process," not to make decisions *for* students. We need to collaborate with students, families, and communities regularly and proactively in ways that promote agency and ownership.

Concrete Ways to Foster Empowerment

- Use modes of learning that center student voice, such as problem-based learning, inquiry learning, or negotiated curriculum.
- Involve students in decision making for school-wide policies or events. Ensure that there are student spots (with full membership rights and responsibilities) on any school-wide committees, in focus groups, and on school boards. Provide mentorship and skill building to support youth success in these roles.
- Collaborate with youth-led organizations in your community, such as youth-led activism collectives and arts organizations.

Connection

Children's emotional well-being and resilience are fostered through their healthy relationships with caring adults. As child trauma expert Bruce Perry and his coauthor Maia Szalavitz put it, "What works to heal [traumatized children] is anything that increases the number and quality of a child's relationships" (2017, p. 260). These relationships must not be limited to the one between student and teacher but should also be encouraged between students and other students, service providers, community members, and so on. Students should also be encouraged to develop the connections between themselves and the world through academic and interest-based avenues. We can help students see themselves reflected in art or literature. We can facilitate student participation in community life and government. Chapter 6 dives much deeper into how teachers can be connection makers and foster relationships.

Unfortunately, schools are often structured to withhold relationship-building opportunities from students unless they misbehave enough to "qualify" for them. I have observed schools that use one-on-one time with a paraprofessional or counselor as a "reward" for good behavior during class time—this is backwards. For children to feel safe and supported enough to engage in academic work, we need first to build relationships, not withhold them. Students shouldn't need to be identified for certain tiers of support in order to spend meaningful time with caring adults in school. This universal principle of connection means that we make it a priority to do whatever it takes to increase the number and strength of relationships for *all* students instead of waiting for something to go wrong first.

To be proactive about connection, schools can dedicate time and structure in the weekly schedule. Some schools use multiage classrooms (e.g., combined second and third grade) with multiple teachers so that students build relationships over two years with the same two adults. Others have teachers "loop" with the same group of students over multiple years, so that students aren't starting over with a new teacher each fall.

I worked with one school, whose mascot is the panda, that has weekly "Panda Pack" time. Panda Packs have nine students—one in each grade, kindergarten through eighth—and one teacher. In these meetings, students work on passion projects based on an area of interest, with older students supporting younger ones. It's a beautiful way to create feelings of connection across the community, not just within classes. It also ensures that students maintain a connection with at least one adult across their entire school experience: students stay in the same Panda Pack from kindergarten through eighth grade. This is only one strategy among many this school uses to build connections within its community. The strongest evidence of their success was when I sat down with a group of students and asked them to choose one word to describe their school. Almost every student in the group said "safe."

Many high schools use advisory time to create small groups that stay connected to one another and to the same teacher for all four years. Advisories have the potential for powerful relationship building, but only when used intentionally for that purpose. Some schools use advisory time simply for announcements or scheduling intervention time, which doesn't do much to enhance relationship and connection. Schools using advisory time more intentionally use these small groups to talk about social issues, process community challenges or current events, and contribute to school-wide decision making. The teacher who serves as the adviser in each of these groups serves as an advocate for the students in her group, creating connections with parents, families, and caregivers, helping students navigate school challenges, and serving as a trusted adult. By building in these multiyear structures for maintaining relationships, schools ensure that students are not treated as interchangeable. Instead, students can be seen and known.

Connection isn't just about relationships within schools; it's also about schools' connections to and place in communities. Teachers and school leaders should regularly collaborate with community groups and individuals, both bringing community members into school and meeting students and families in the community.

Concrete Ways to Foster Connection
- Implement an advisory structure so that each student has a relationship "home base" within the school.
- Create connections between the school and community partners. Keep a database of local professionals and community leaders who are willing to host students for field trips or internships or to visit classrooms. Solicit ideas and additional partnerships from families and caregivers.
- Don't forget fun and joy. Relationships thrive when kids can be kids together, be silly, and develop inside jokes and shared memories. Slow down and enjoy the goofy moments.

Predictability

Trauma creates a profound sense of unpredictability. Traumatic events occur in unpredictable ways. Once impacted by trauma, children become highly attuned to cues of danger, and their stress-response systems are activated more easily. These cues may trigger the stress-response system unconsciously, which means that trauma-affected children may not feel that their own moods or emotions are predictable, let alone the outside world. Living with a sense of chaos can worsen children's perceptions of the world being an unsafe place.

Being predictable doesn't mean being rigid. (Spoiler alert: the fourth proactive priority is flexibility.) We need to consider the interplay of predictability and flexibility for any structures or routines we build. Despite the rigid schedule of many schools, they can be an unpredictable place for students. Some of this has to do with inconsistencies between teaching staff and students experiencing different rules, different environments, and different responses to their behavior in each room of a school. Some of it is simply due to the unpredictable nature of many humans gathering together in the same place each day.

One of the universal supports we can offer students to make school feel more predictable is getting on the same page as adults. To provide predictable responses to students, we also need to make sure that as adults we stay regulated and do not become emotionally volatile in the face of student challenges. Predictable responses from adults help kids stay safe. Chapter 9 talks more about structures that help adults stay grounded in the work and therefore more predictable in responses to students.

Another aspect of predictability is in anticipating the moments that feel unsettled and planning to give time and space to settle. Think about your students coming back from recess or lunch or returning to class after an assembly. You have two choices at that moment: ignore the fact that most students will feel unsettled, attempt to get them straight to work, and then feel frustrated when they aren't on-task immediately; or anticipate that people's bodies and minds feel unsettled when moving from task to task or activity to activity and predictably build in a settling routine before moving to academic tasks. A settling routine could be as simple as a few moments for students to chit-chat, get seated, drink water, and use the bathroom. It could be more structured, with stretching, movement, or breathing led by the teacher. Either way, planning in routines that address the needs of our minds and bodies can help foster a sense of predictability and calm.

I was once invited to a school where teachers asked me if some of their students' challenging behaviors could be related to underlying

trauma. In my visit at the school, I observed many classrooms throughout several days. I saw students as young as second grade working for
long stretches of time on individual laptops; large groups of students
asked to sit still, elbow to elbow on a bench, and listen for twenty
minutes to verbal instructions; one short recess in the middle of the
day with very few movement breaks; no group projects; and very little
hands-on learning. Here's what I made of this observation: Could some
of the challenging behaviors described by teachers be attributable to
trauma? Sure. But the same behaviors were mostly perfectly developmentally appropriate behavior for children who are asked to keep their
bodies still and quiet for hours on end.

Children need to move. Children need to be engaged in meaningful, relevant work. There's a saying, "If it's predictable, it's preventable."
One of the most predictable things in a school is that children have
bodies and that they need to move their bodies. They will do this with
or without a structured opportunity (like recess) from adults. We can
foster wellness through being consistent in our expectations, in our
structures, and in our view of students as human.

Concrete Ways to Foster Predictability

- Create flexible routines for the school day. Thoughtfully schedule pull-out services or groups so that students don't deviate too
  much from the overall class schedule for the day.
- Plan in time to settle after transitions and for students (and
  teachers) to move their bodies and meet basic needs. "Bell-to-bell
  instruction" with three minutes between classes is inhumane.
- Teachers are a great source of predictability when we can remain
  grounded and regulated throughout a school day. Teachers
  should consider what coping and mindfulness strategies they can
  use during stressful moments, and administrators should focus
  on creating sustainable working conditions for all school staff.

Flexibility

Trauma impacts each person differently. Trauma can also impact
the same person differently from day to day. Because we can end up

extrasensitive to the cues in our environment and go into survival mode at a moment's notice, people with trauma need flexibility so that they can feel their feelings and not feel rushed and out of control because they're trying to fit into someone else's schedule.

One size never fits all in education, and that's particularly true when we think about mental health. When we feel pressured to fit into a rigid schedule and meet other people's expectations with no sensitivity for our emotions, we can end up dissociating and shutting down our ability to stay in tune with our minds and bodies. Dissociation is a stress response in which we feel distant from the current moment (Perry & Szalavitz, 2017). It's the feeling of watching yourself from outside of your own body, like what's happening isn't actually real. When we ask students to rush, to ignore their feelings so they can "be positive" in class, in essence we are asking them to dissociate. Members of the school community shouldn't need to compartmentalize in order to be a valued part of the school.

Instead, we should have opportunities to check in and notice what we need. We should be able to do things in different ways because the learning goal is more important than the standardized process of getting there. The phrase I encourage teachers to remember is "there are different paths up the mountain." We might all be hiking to the same place, but some of us will need more breaks or to walk at a slower pace. Some of us may wander off the path to explore an interesting part of the forest we noticed along the hike. Some of us may want to walk alone while others need to follow a guide. The key is to identify what's truly important and let go of how tightly we hold on to how and when students get there.

For example, many teachers (myself definitely included) have certain activities or lessons that we just love teaching. These lessons aren't the only way to meet the academic standard, but for whatever reason we're attached. For me, I absolutely love a "research talk" activity I do with my writing students where they give mini presentations on their research topics to peers. If I have a student whose anxiety is an insurmountable barrier to an in-class presentation, I need to be flexible in how students meet the learning target. This means I have to let go of my own excitement about the actual activity and remind myself about the learning goals, allowing for a different path up the mountain. In a recent semester, I had just this situation and worked with the student to help him understand the goals of the assignment; in this case he was to be able to articulate his research in the frame of "what, so what, and now what" and to get peer feedback on this. Through conversation with the student, we came up with alternative times and smaller group settings to do his research talk.

It's usually fairly simple to make these types of accommodations for students, but many teachers hesitate to do so because it "wouldn't be fair" or because we are attached to the way we envision the lesson going. Be proactive with your students in building a shared understanding of the importance of our flexibility and grace for one another, and a shared value that fairness isn't as important as supporting one another with what we each need.

Flexibility is also essential in the realm of discipline. As discussed in Chapter 2, zero-tolerance policies harm students and contribute to the school-to-prison pipeline. If our student handbooks and discipline codes are full of inflexible if-then consequences for a laundry list of student infractions, they aren't trauma-informed or equity-centered.

Concrete Ways to Foster Flexibility

- Use pedagogical approaches like competency-based learning or proficiency-based learning. These approaches focus on students demonstrating their progress toward learning outcomes, with less emphasis on completing certain activities or amounts of seat time. The principles of universal design for learning (UDL; see Chapter 4) are also a helpful guide in providing flexible opportunities for access and expression.
- Recognize your own pet peeves. We all have rules that we cling more tightly to, not because they're more important than others but because they just bother us. I really dislike when people are late, so my impulse is to dock students for being late to class. That impulse doesn't serve me or my students well. Instead, I moved to starting each class with a group check-in that students are motivated to participate in. Students want to be on time, and

if they run a few minutes late, they don't miss crucial instruction. Letting go of my pet peeve costs me nothing and helps build a culture of flexibility and trust.

Putting the Four Priorities Together

There are inherent tensions between these four proactive priorities. It isn't easy to be both predictable and flexible, for example. When we relinquish our control in the classroom in our effort to be empowering, it can be messy to rebuild new structures that rely on fostering classroom communities in which teachers share power with students.

The most helpful way I use the four priorities is to guide my own reflective practice. When designing something new, I ask myself:

- Is this predictable?
- Is it flexible?
- Does it foster empowerment?
- Does it foster connection?

Answering these questions helps me improve my classroom design. This was helpful when my college moved to online instruction midsemester due to the COVID-19 pandemic. No road map was provided on how to pivot to online instruction during a global health crisis. As I sat down to plan the remaining weeks of my course, I revisited the academic goals of the course and what I had thought I would do to help students meet those goals. With some sadness, I let go of some of the cool in-class activities and projects I had hoped we would do. Then, working from the four questions above, I designed what I hoped would give students flexibility and predictability while keeping us connected and allowing for their choice and agency in meeting our goals.

I highlighted important assignments and was transparent about what was required (predictability), while letting students adjust due dates and have some wiggle room on expectations like page-length requirements (flexibility). I created a group check-in space in our online class and also set up individual phone calls with each student (connection).

As I always do, I invited students to self-assess their final grade and facilitated an activity where students wrote to our college president to give feedback on the school's response to COVID-19 (empowerment).

Consider the four proactive priorities a starting point for your decision making while you also put your equity literacy into practice. In my pandemic class planning, I also paid attention to the structural components of critical wellness by providing students resources about accessing food assistance and mini grants from the college to help with internet access. I used my position of influence as a faculty member to advocate for equity-driven choices from the administration, like implementing a pass-fail option for all students during the crisis. Although I could not single-handedly fix all of the challenges my students faced, I tried to address issues at the personal and systemic levels from within my role. The rest of the semester wasn't perfect—I doubt anyone's pandemic planning was—but many of my students thanked me at the end of the semester for my flexibility and for demonstrating that I cared about them as people first and students second.

Even so, I still think of all the different ways I could have approached the situation. Would some of them have resulted in stronger final projects and academic achievement for my students? Probably. But as Bettina Love wrote, "If students are not well, test scores do not matter" (2019, p. 160). Returning to the guiding focus on humanization, wellness, and thriving as universal goals for all my students, with the four priorities to guide my thinking, helps me navigate complex situations.

Instead of turning away from the difficulties, we instead need to embrace the complexity. This requires that we continually check our understanding and stay up-to-date with new developments in the field, not getting stuck in an outdated framework. It requires that we set aside time for reflection and ask ourselves whether the strategies and decisions we've made are working for our students and whether they align with our evolving understanding. Embracing complexity requires that we be vulnerable enough to say "I don't know" and to listen to the perspectives of those who are frequently silenced, especially our students and their caregivers. It's messy—but embracing the mess is how we grow.

ACTION STEPS

How to use the four proactive priorities will be different for everyone, depending on your current practice, your role, your students, and your school. The Four Proactive Priorities Reflection exercise in Table 5.1 will help you consider how you currently foster predictability, flexibility, connection, and empowerment.

Table 5.1: Exercise: Four Proactive Priorities Reflection

For each proactive priority, write down what you consider your strengths and challenges in implementation. Consider sharing with a peer who can help you create goals or action steps from this reflection. Revisit your reflections from time to time to see how your understanding and implementation of these priorities have grown and developed.

Predictability	
Strengths—What Am I Doing Well?	**Challenges or Opportunities to Grow**
Interactions/relationships	Interactions/relationships
Pedagogy/academics	Pedagogy/academics
Systems/policy/school-wide	Systems/policy/school-wide

Flexibility	
Strengths—What Am I Doing Well?	**Challenges or Opportunities to Grow**
Interactions/relationships	Interactions/relationships
Pedagogy/academics	Pedagogy/academics
Systems/policy/school-wide	Systems/policy/school-wide

Connection	
Strengths—What Am I Doing Well?	**Challenges or Opportunities to Grow**
Interactions/relationships	Interactions/relationships
Pedagogy/academics	Pedagogy/academics
Systems/policy/school-wide	Systems/policy/school-wide
Empowerment	
Strengths—What Am I Doing Well?	**Challenges or Opportunities to Grow**
Interactions/relationships	Interactions/relationships
Pedagogy/academics	Pedagogy/academics
Systems/policy/school-wide	Systems/policy/school-wide

Part III

Shift 2: Rethink Your Role as an Educator

It was a chilly day in October, and Gabriel wasn't wearing socks. Heather, his third-grade teacher, noticed that Gabriel showed up to school most days wearing tennis shoes but no socks. She mentioned this to a coworker, who said, "Oh, his family just moved here from Puerto Rico. Maybe he doesn't have socks at home." *Poor Gabriel,* Heather thought, *it must be embarrassing not to have socks. I bet I can help.* Heather prided herself on going the extra mile for her students, so on her way home from school she stopped at Target and picked up a few packs of socks, which she gave to Gabriel the next day. He seemed confused as he accepted them.

The following morning Gabriel's mom, Daniela, brought him to school and asked to speak with the teacher. Heather was stunned when Daniela, clearly upset, explained that Gabriel had plenty of socks but, like many eight-year-olds, simply goofed around in the morning and didn't always follow his mother's instructions for getting dressed. "I'm a nurse, and mornings are busy in our house. You would know that if you had tried to get to know us instead of assuming what my son needs," Daniela said.

In the process of trying to be helpful, Heather actually damaged her relationship with her student and his family. Regardless of Heather's good intentions, her impact was a negative one. Would things have gone differently if Heather had built a strong relationship with Gabriel and Daniela? Maybe, but relationship building on its own isn't a silver bullet. Heather still needs to address the assumptions and biases that led her to the conclusion that this family was needy instead of to the question, What's going on for my student, and how might I find out?

A savior mentality is when we see our job description as rescuing broken kids or compensating for broken homes. This mindset rests on the faulty premise that the obstacles to a child's education can be solved by fixing the student instead of fixing the conditions that create the obstacles. As Heather learned the hard way, when we focus on fixing kids, we often find problems that aren't even there.

Approaching our work with a savior mentality perpetuates rather than heals trauma. We need to shift from a savior mentality to *unconditional positive regard, a mindset that focuses on the inherent skills, capacities, and value of every student.* Educators shouldn't aim to heal, fix, or save but to be connection makers and just one of many caring adults in a child's life.

This shift helps to move us closer to these principles of equity-centered trauma-informed education:

- **Principle 2: Asset based**—Trauma-informed education is asset based and doesn't attempt to fix kids, because kids are not broken. Instead, it addresses the conditions, systems, and structures that harm kids.
- **Principle 4: Human centered**—Trauma-informed education means centering our shared humanity.

In Part III, Chapter 6 explores how relationships can heal but also harm and unpack the dangers of a savior mentality. Chapter 7 then describes unconditional positive regard and how it supports equity-centered trauma-informed environments. Finally, Chapter 8 addresses the necessity of boundaries to keep both students and teachers safe.

6 | Build Relationships
Rooted in Equity

Search for advice on building trauma-informed classrooms, and you will encounter one word over and over: *relationships.* Trauma-informed education experts, researchers, and clinicians agree: healing from trauma and building resilience to guard against future trauma happens within the context of strong, supportive relationships. Children's feelings of positive well-being have been associated with their sense of belonging and connectedness with school (Watson, 2017). Students who feel emotionally supported by their teachers do better with their academic work and their social-emotional health (Guess & Bowling, 2014). In our work toward equity and social justice, relationships are essential in building affirming, empowering environments for students who have traditionally been marginalized at school (Milner, 2015; Hammond, 2015; Minor, 2019). We need to truly see and know students for who they are as full people. To create equitable and trauma-informed schools, we need to learn about and affirm our students and their values, interests, and strengths.

Proactively building relationships sets us up for success. Relationships can also help us navigate hard times. In the context of trauma recovery, relationships can mediate the impacts of trauma and provide healing opportunities. Recall from Chapter 5 Bruce Perry and Maia Szalavitz's statement that, "The research on the most effective treatment to help child trauma victims might be accurately summed up this way: what works best is anything that increases the quality and number of relationships in a child's life" (2017, p. 85). Caring adults don't need to be trained therapists or trauma counselors. The relationships Perry references include parents, teachers, coaches, neighbors, aunts and uncles, spiritual and religious leaders, Scout leaders, community elders, and anyone else who can play a consistent role in a child's life. These connections create a feeling of safety in which children are comfortable enough to take risks, explore, and learn new things (Craig, 2017). Trauma-affected children sometimes lag behind their peers in their social and emotional functioning because they are focused on keeping themselves safe. For children to practice and develop these skills, they need trusting and sustained relationships.

So, there's no doubt: relationships are important. Most educators already know this. But what should these relationships look like in an equity-centered trauma-informed school? What does it mean to build relationships in a context in which the two parties are inherently on unequal footing? How much should we engage with students' emotional lives, given that we're not mental health professionals? These are questions that go unanswered when we simply advise teachers to "build relationships." After all, not all relationships are supportive or, in Perry and Szalavitz's words, "quality." And understanding the need for relationships doesn't always translate into action. Many schools leave relationship building up to individual teachers while also creating conditions that make relationship building difficult, such as large classes sizes, short class periods, and expectations that teachers engage in academic instruction "from bell to bell."

Most of us can remember at least one teacher who changed our lives for the better because that teacher saw who we were and who we could become, affirming us and supporting us. Many of us can also remember at least one teacher who dismissed us or told us we were destined for failure. I know which type of teacher I want to be, and to become that powerfully supportive adult in my students' lives, I need to be intentional in my relationship building.

Relationships can heal, but relationships can also harm. As teachers sometimes we exert our position of power in the classroom to control our students, like when we dismiss their concerns or tell them to "do this because I'm the teacher and I said so." We can fall into a savior mentality that diminishes our students' and their families' inherent value, like when we assume that a struggling student has a terrible home life without ever actually getting to know her. We sometimes allow racism, homophobia, sexism, and other forms of bias to cloud our ability to clearly see our students' strengths and assets. We can end up blurring boundaries, creating confusion and harm for vulnerable students.

All of these missteps are harmful, even when based on good intentions. The consequences of these missteps can be long lasting and life changing. Students' academic records can influence access to higher education and jobs. The labels we give students can shape how they seem themselves. And of course, there are the consequences of trauma caused in classrooms and by teachers. The stakes are high, so we need more guidance than simply "build relationships."

For student-teacher relationships to be trauma-informed and equity-centered, teachers need to see relationship building as a skill set to learn and practice. There are requisite skills and competencies I need as a teacher to be a force for equity and justice. I need to build self-awareness of the social dynamics at play in student-teacher relationships. I need to choose to intentionally approach my students with unconditional acceptance. I need to build and maintain healthy boundaries. I need to develop my critical awareness and equity literacy so that I understand the full context of how oppression intersects with education for my marginalized students (López, 2017).

Teachers can't do this alone or through sheer force of will. School structures need to shift and leaders need to provide time, training, and resources for teachers to develop these skills and competencies. There need to be changes in things like the bell schedule, student-teacher ratio, and communication structures to support relationship building. Continue to hold that system-wide lens in your mind as you read the chapters in this part, which focus on things that are directly within the realm of influence for all teachers: our own mindset and orientation toward student-teacher relationships. Part IV discusses how to talk with school leaders and revisits whole-school approaches.

Unpacking Deficit Views and Savior Mentality

"Jeremie has so much trauma, I don't think it's fair to keep him in a class where his needs aren't being met." I heard these words from a special education teacher in a meeting about trauma-informed practices, at a school where I was consulting. The special educator looked at me imploringly, hoping I would back her up in front of her principal. On the surface it might seem like her statement was empathetic or intended to garner support for Jeremie, the six-year-old child about whom she professed to be so worried. But when I hear teachers talk about kids with "so much trauma," they are often focusing on the challenging behavior or academic failure of these same students. By placing trauma at the core of these explanations, as teachers we distance ourselves from our responsibility to create safe and affirming classroom environments. In other words, if it's the trauma's fault that Jeremie is struggling, it can't be my fault.

Simply put, deficit views are those that focus on what students are lacking and the ways they need to be helped. In conversations about equity, deficit explanations point to children, their families, and their perceived cultures as the reason for inequity, rather than the structures or conditions that actually create and sustain the inequity. For example, how do we explain the underrepresentation of women in science, technology, engineering, and mathematics (STEM) careers? The deficit explanation of this gender imbalance is that women just aren't as interested in or skilled at STEM subjects. This places the blame on women and girls and not on the structures and systems that prevent their success in STEM careers. Some of those structures and systems include the stereotypes and gender norms that lead adults to discourage girls from STEM opportunities, and the sexual harassment and discrimination that prevent women from advancing to STEM leadership roles.

Why does it matter how we explain inequity? Our mindset shapes how we build relationships, and those relationships can foster student success or impede it. Holding deficit mindsets toward our students lowers our expectations, and this in turn lowers student achievement (Wang et al., 2018). This self-fulfilling prophecy disproportionately affects children of color and leads to concrete disparities in schools, such as restricting access to more challenging curricula (López, 2017). Deficit mindsets contribute to academic inequities.

Deficit views tend to fall apart under close scrutiny, because they're based on stereotypes, not on facts. Take, for example, the myth that some parents just don't value learning. In summarizing the research on parent involvement in education, Paul Gorski wrote: "Studies have demonstrated consistently that people experiencing poverty value education just as much as wealthy people *despite* often experiencing schools as unwelcoming and inequitable" (2018, p. 74). So if there is no evidence that this is the truth, why does the belief persist among teachers? Deficit views don't suddenly appear out of nowhere; they are shaped by messages of American meritocracy, by racism, and by beliefs about class. To dislodge deficit views, we need to interrogate and unpack these messages.

PRACTICE YOUR EQUITY-CENTERED TRAUMA-INFORMED LENS: HIDDEN MESSAGES

Teachers are on the receiving end of quite a lot of messages about our role in students' lives, so we have a lot of unpacking to do. If you're a teacher, you've likely heard messages like "teachers create the leaders of tomorrow," or have been told that you're a saint, or seen a motivational TED talk that just *one* teacher can turn a student's life around. These messages might sound inspirational on the surface, but they can foster deficit views and savior mentality.

Let's practice our equity-centered trauma-informed critical thinking. A quote I see making its rounds on social media every couple of months is attributed to a prominent teaching personality: "Students who are loved at home come to school to learn, and students who aren't come to school to be loved." What are the deficit messages you see hidden in quotes like these?

When I'm unpacking a potential problematic message, I start by asking questions. Here are a few questions I have about this quote:

- Don't all students want to learn? Aren't all kids naturally curious?

- Don't all kids (and people, really) want to be loved?
- Does this quote suggest that a teacher's love and a parent's love are the same thing?
- Do kids have a choice about why (or whether) they come to school?
- Are there really a whole lot of parents who don't love their kids?
- What effect does it have on my teaching practice if I believe my students' parents don't love them?
- How does one tell the difference between a parent who doesn't love their kids and a parent who loves their kids but is overwhelmed or underresourced and struggles to effectively parent?
- How does one tell the difference between a kid who is loved at home and one who isn't?
- Do loved kids always want to learn?
- Should I lower my academic expectations for "unloved" kids because they're just here to be loved?
- Does trauma happen only to kids in "unloving" households?
- Does being loved at home affect motivation for learning?
- What would my students' parents think if they saw me tweet or post this quote? (adapted from Venet, 2019a)

This quote is just one such message among many similar ones on social media and in education books. Use critical questions to unveil hidden messages before hitting the "share button."

The Road to Savior Mentality

How does deficit view transform into a savior mentality? It happens when teachers, who hold a position of power, combine the faulty logic of deficit view with good intentions, leading us to "help" in ways that don't actually help, like Heather did in the scenario described in the introduction to Part III.

To see how this happens, we have to recognize how deficit views can hide in plain sight, masked with "kindness." At the community college where I teach, I have many students who migrated to the United States from countries in Africa and the Middle East. Many of these students began learning English as adults and do not yet have fluency in academic English conventions. I have had instances when I recognized that I was doing a student a disservice by lowering my expectations for academic writing because I was trying not to be too harsh in my feedback. This came from a "well-meaning" place: I recognized all of the hardships that these students faced as a result of their migrant status, and it made me want to highlight the good in their work and not focus just on what was "wrong" in their writing. The result: my students didn't receive meaningful feedback from me and missed out on the opportunity to grow that other students received. What good was I doing these students by lowering my expectations?

Fighting deficit views of students means actively choosing to see their inherent strengths, capacity, and potential. It also means understanding the sociopolitical and historical context that creates barriers and challenges for our students. By developing my own critical awareness and equity literacy, I came to realize that my well-meaning "kindness" was actually rooted in a deficit view. If I were being honest with myself, what I actually feared was that my English-learning students would not be able to manage feedback or meet the academic expectations I held for my other students. If I truly believe in all students' capacity and inherent ability, I will communicate this through providing high levels of support to meet my high expectations. Now, I try to embrace social scientist Brené Brown's aphorism "clear is kind." Brown's (2018) research into vulnerability found that many people avoid having hard conversations or giving feedback because they fear coming across as unkind. I know this was true for me: I didn't want to come across as uncaring to my migrant students. In reality, withholding feedback and creating confusion because we are afraid of conflict is *unkind*. My lowered expectations for English-learning students were unkind, even though I told myself my intentions were good. I know that my migrant students face more barriers and obstacles on their way to mastery of academic English. I don't need to be one of those barriers by withholding valuable academic instruction.

My missteps with my migrant students demonstrate how a deficit view can easily transform into savior mentality. The deficit logic went something like this: Because my students experienced trauma and hardship, they must be damaged; because they are damaged, they must not be able to handle feedback; because they can't handle it, I will rescue them from facing more hardship by going easy on them. In making these leaps of logic, I skipped over important steps, like checking on my bias and assumptions and actually talking to my students. Like Heather did when she jumped to action to buy socks for Gabriel, I jumped to a harmful conclusion when I wrote "Great first draft" on a student's paper instead of addressing the academic writing concerns.

Teachers need to let go of the savior mentality because, by stepping into the role of the rescuer, we leave our students no role but to be the rescued. If we define our success by how many individual kids we save, we also lose sight of the structures and systems that need to change to help *all* kids.

The shift away from savior mentality is necessary to do equity-centered trauma-informed work. Recall from Chapter 4 that the heart of the universal approach is embracing our full humanity and the full humanity of our students. Carla Shalaby, educator and author of *Troublemakers: Lessons in Freedom From Young People at School* (2017), wrote that "schools are trying to make people, but these young people insist they are already made" (p. 159). Shalaby argued that the students who are often labeled troublemakers are like canaries in the coal mine, showing us what is wrong with the metaphorical (and sometimes literal) air quality in our schools. Students who disrupt, act out, or don't fit in aren't inherently challenging as people. They are asserting their freedom. Categorizing their behavior as challenging says more about us as teachers than about the students themselves. Our task as teachers is to affirm the fullness of our students as people who matter instead of labeling and excluding those who seem not to fit with how we "do school." All too often, teachers focus on what students are lacking and try to change the kids rather than looking at what the environment and classroom are lacking and try to change ourselves.

Turning Inward: Addressing Bias

Savior mentality, trauma, and teaching get even more tangled when we layer in race and identity. Eight in 10 public school teachers are white, and around 75% are women. In contrast, a little more than half of all public school students are Black, Indigenous, and students of color (National Center for Education Statistics, 2019). This means that teachers are mostly white women, and increasingly, our students are mostly Black, Indigenous, and other children of color. As equity-centered trauma-informed teachers, we must consider what these dynamics mean for our work.

In reflecting on instances of racism in school throughout her childhood, teacher and author Lorena Germán wrote: "What I learned is that White supremacy doesn't just look like White men, real scary-like, in robes, with pitchforks, violently screaming racial slurs at us. But it can look like White women who don't care. Who don't listen. Who are there to collect their pay check and see their 'tough love' in our communities as charity" (2020, para. 7). White teachers, no matter our good intentions, can cause harm to students of color.

Trauma-informed practice isn't inherently a deficit view, but it becomes one when we use "trauma" as a proxy for "those damaged kids." White teachers need to critically examine why we are interested in trauma-informed practices. Are we drawn to this because it provides an explanation for why the kids misbehave and offers a promise of solutions to "fix" them? If so, that's a white savior mindset that will continue to do harm.

Practically speaking, we can begin to rid ourselves of a savior mentality by noticing and interrupting deficit narratives. This is part of our ongoing development of equity literacy. In other parts of this book I discussed the importance of understanding systems, history, and sociopolitical context. We also have to turn this understanding inward and examine our own attitudes and assumptions. One framework for understanding this is implicit bias.

Implicit bias refers to the unconscious associations that we make, based on the thousands of social messages we receive throughout our lives. Teachers so often are in a rush and need to make snap decisions, and our implicit bias comes into play when we do (Staats, 2016). As we are constantly deciding how to respond to students' questions, comments, and behavior, we should also reflect on how these decisions are informed by our beliefs.

In a study conducted in 2014 at the Center on Poverty and Inequality at Georgetown Law, researchers surveyed adults about traits associated with Black girls at various ages. They found that the adults interviewed believed that, compared to white girls of the same age, Black girls are less innocent, know more about adult topics, and need less nurturing (Epstein et al., 2017). Researchers connected this "adultification" of Black girls to cultural stereotypes and prejudices against Black women.

If this view of Black girls as "more adult" than their white peers is among teachers' unconscious associations about their students, how might that impact how they react to Black girls' behavior in the moment? How might these associations inform their response to a Black girl, for example, rolling her eyes? I don't have to wonder about the answers to these questions: the same study reported that Black girls are disproportionately disciplined, referred to law enforcement, and suspended from school compared to their white peers. Given the negative impact of school discipline and the school-to-prison pipeline, we can't say we're trauma-informed educators if we allow these patterns to persist.

Teacher bias can also directly cause trauma when it is expressed in microaggressions. According to psychologist Thema Bryant-Davis, "Microaggressions are intentional or unintentional brief acts of subtle or covert bias and discrimination aimed at persons from targeted groups, which may trigger memories of pas individual or collective acts of oppression" (2018, p. 86). A microaggression can be a small comment, like asking a person of color, "But where are you *really* from?" Microaggressions can be looks or gestures, like a white person clutching her belongings closer when a Black teen walks by. Microaggressions can even sound "nice" or complimentary, like when a teacher says to a gay student she doesn't know well, "You're always so fashionable," or a straight girl calls him "my new gay best friend." When seemingly "nice" comments reinforce stereotypes and reduce people to tokens, they do harm. Even though these interactions may look small, their impact is large.

Microaggressions can impact marginalized people in two interlocking ways. First, experiencing a constant stream of microaggressions can undermine a person's sense of physical and psychological safety, and trying to cope with a constantly unsafe environment is traumatic (Nadal, 2018, pp. xiv, 150). Students who expend their energy at school surviving the threat that comes with the presence of others' bias are being robbed of their opportunity to focus instead on academics. For example, Sara, a high school student who uses a wheelchair, faces a stream of ableist microaggressions all day at school. First, her bus driver talks to her like a small child while operating the wheelchair lift: "Just wait one more minute sweetie, while I get this set up." Next, while hurrying to get to class on time, a classmate starts to push Sara's wheelchair without consent: "Let me help you!" On arriving to class, Sara's teacher is introducing a "diversity book" unit and proudly says she has curated a collection of novels with "all kinds of people." Sara browses through the choices and can't find a single book with a disabled protagonist. The result of these constant microaggressions: Sara's mind is occupied with avoiding harm, proving her worth, and managing her frustration as she navigates her day. Sara doesn't have equitable access to her education because of this.

The second impact of microaggressions is in their ability to trigger. Microaggressions can connect to historical community trauma and elicit painful memories that trigger the stress response (Bryant-Davis, 2018). For example, a microaggression I hear sometimes as a Jewish person is when others joke about Jews being responsible for killing Jesus. While the joke itself doesn't necessarily mean that harm is imminent for me, hearing it often brings to mind memories of all of the other times I have been made to feel unsafe because of my Judaism, echoing the generational trauma of my people killed because of beliefs like the ones being joked about. The presence of a microaggression says, "Don't forget that you're different. Don't forget you're not one of us." When we consider relationship building as teachers, we have to recognize that these moments can have powerful repercussions, impacting our ability to build true trusting relationships. To be equity-centered and trauma-informed, we must build relationships that are affirming, not harmful.

The opposite of deficit views isn't simply to "think positive" or "be kind." To build authentic relationships from a strengths-based place, we must interrogate our assumptions, learn about the lives and experiences of our students, and choose to reject a savior mentality.

ACTION STEPS

Letting go of savior mentality requires self-reflection and development of our equity literacy. Here are some starting points for this work:

Develop Your Lens

- Savior mentality thrives when we ignore the inherent strengths and capacities of our students. Think about current or past students whom you felt especially drawn to help. For each student, make a list of that student's strengths and internal resources. What are survival skills and traits of resilience that your students possess, regardless of your intervention? Make a habit of noticing these strengths in new students that you meet.
- Practice your critical lens when using social media. When you see memes, inspirational quotes, or generalizations about trauma-affected students, try making a list of questions like the list for the quote about how students who are not loved at home come to school (just) to be loved. Start by asking, *What are the assumptions being made here?* and expand from there. The practice of questioning is a foundation of my own reflective practice.

Transform Your Classroom

- To put your equity literacy into practice, ask a colleague to help you conduct an equity review of your classroom. Invite your colleague to observe while you teach and note whom you call on, which students you check in with or discipline, and where you seem to focus your attention. Gather data from your classroom, such as office referrals and grades. Finally, create a list of your students with relevant information about race, gender, special education status, and free and reduced lunch status (a marker for family income). With your colleague, look for patterns. What do you notice? What do you wonder? How do the patterns in your classroom reflect those in school-wide data? If you've identified any disproportionate patterns, such as calling more frequently on girls or disciplining your students with IEPs more often, make a plan about how you will address this moving forward.

Shift the Systems

- Sometimes we can fall into a savior role when we don't trust the systems of support in our school or community. For example, Heather, who bought socks for her student, assumed that the only way students could access additional clothes would be for her to buy them. When there are barrier-free ways for students and families to opt into support, we can take pressure off of ourselves as individuals. One school I visited had a family resource room near the school entrance. The room is open whenever school is open, and families can simply drop in to pick up food, clothing, books, and other resources. There's no need to sign up, apply, or justify why you're in need. This creates an easy and nonshaming way for families and students to access support and means that individual teachers do not need to compensate for a lack of resources.

7 | Cultivate Unconditional Positive Regard

As a teacher, I know how important it is to create clear expectations for my students and hold them to high standards. This also applies to me as I seek to build relationships with my students. The high standards I hold myself to in building teacher-student relationships come from my guiding philosophy: unconditional positive regard. This approach helps ground my equity-centered and trauma-informed work.

The term *unconditional positive regard* was coined by psychologist Carl R. Rogers, who developed an approach called client-centered psychotherapy. Here's how Rogers described unconditional positive regard:

> *It means that there are no conditions of acceptance, no feeling of "I like you only if you are thus and so." . . . It means a caring for the client, but not in a possessive way or in such a way as simply to satisfy the therapist's own needs. It means a caring for the client as a separate person, with permission to have his own feelings, his own experiences. One client describes the therapist as "fostering my possession of my own experience . . . that [this] is my experience and that I am actually having it: thinking what I think, feeling what I feel, wanting what I want, fearing what I fear: no 'ifs,' 'buts,' or 'not reallys.'"* (1957, p. 4)

Unconditional positive regard isn't limited to a therapeutic approach: Alfie Kohn (2005) built on Rogers's work with the concept "unconditional teaching" to apply unconditional positive regard to the classroom. Kohn argued that schools promote a kind of conditional acceptance when they elevate achievement and obedience rather than building community and relationships. Unconditional teachers accept students for who they are, not what they do.

Unconditional positive regard is a stance I take in relationship to my students. The message of unconditional positive regard is, "I care about you. You have value. You don't have to do anything to prove it to me, and nothing's going to change my mind." I sometimes try to imagine myself radiating unconditional positive regard like a glow around me when I walk into a classroom. But I also actually say those words to my students in ways that fit our relationship. I make sure to tell them I care about them, regardless of what they accomplish or achieve in our academic work together. This care infuses all of my teaching choices, from personal interactions to learning design. Importantly, unconditional positive regard stands in opposition to savior mentality and deficit thinking. Table 7.1 contrasts deficit and savior views with unconditional mentality.

Table 7.1: Deficit and Savior Mentality Versus Unconditional Mentality	
Deficit/savior mentality	**Unconditional mentality**
I am here to save you.	I am here to support you.
My students are not capable of helping themselves. I need to save them.	My students are in charge of their own lives. I am here to help them work toward their self-identified goals.
My students with trauma are broken. I feel so bad for those kids.	I witness the struggle of my students and their capacity to heal.
I alone can fix them. I can "be the one."	I recognize the need to work as a team.

My primary goal is to make sure my students can trust me and talk to me.	My primary goal is to make sure my students have people in their lives they can trust and talk to, whether or not that's me.
My value is in how much my students respond to me.	My value is not dependent on how my students respond to me.
Teachers can provide the love students don't get at home.	I don't assume that love has anything to do with trauma, or that trauma happens only at home. I see myself as one caring adult in the life of my students, not the only caring adult.

Building Unconditional Relationships

A philosophy is important, but only as much as we put that philosophy into action. Unconditional positive regard is an equity approach when we actively put it into practice in our everyday interactions with students.

Sometimes unconditional positive regard is just as simple as how we greet our students when they are late to class: how I greet them can communicate either my unconditional care or my lack of regard. If I don't have unconditional positive regard, I might say, "You're late, sit down," and roll my eyes, or I might sarcastically say, "Nice of you to show up." These responses tell students that I care about them only as long as they follow my expectations—they are an inconvenience. Even if I don't mean to communicate this, small moments add up. If students comes to my class and I roll my eyes, if they go into the hallway and are told to take off their hat, if they sit down at lunch and are warned to speak more quietly, then the cumulative message of school is that orderliness is the most important thing.

Instead, I can greet my student with "Hey! It's great to see you today. Settle in a minute and then I'll catch you up." When we work from unconditional positive regard, the message is that I value you for who you are, not what you do or how you do it. This doesn't mean that I won't address attendance issues later, but my priority when my students arrive isn't to scold them about compliance. My priority is to greet them in a way that says they matter and that their presence is more important than how fast they got here.

In general, slowing down most conversations with students to simply ask, "How's it going?" changes the tone of my whole day. When visiting schools as part of my consulting work, it's always surprising to me how infrequently I see teachers stopping to just check in with students throughout the day, or even saying students' names. Creating an environment of care means going back to the basics and not skipping the human connection of just asking one another how we're doing. This may seem like an obvious point to make, but the basis of unconditional positive regard is the phrase "I care about you." To care about someone else means that we see the sum of all of their strengths and challenges and choose to care for them.

Our schools need to be places where we care *for* our students, not just care *about* them. Education philosopher Nel Noddings calls this an "ethic of care," in which learning how to be cared for and learning how to care for others are central tasks of education. Caring *for* students means being in relationship with them, whereas caring *about* students allows us to keep our distance. If we commit to an ethic of care, building relationships and caring for our students aren't strategies in the name of increasing academic achievement but the actual goal itself.

One of the foundations of caring is seeing and truly getting to know our students. Too often our approaches to relationship building in school can feel transactional. I remember that, as a new teacher, my strategy for relationship building was to give students a long survey to complete, telling me about their interests, learning styles, and favorite colors. These types of "getting to know you" surveys are only surface level and don't do much to create a caring relationship. Now I try to get to know students the same way I would get to know a new friend: spending time together, asking questions about their lives and what they feel passionate about, and talking about what matters to us both. Real relationship building isn't flashy and can't be condensed to "fifteen tricks and tips." Sometimes building relationships means sitting together in silence and simply getting used to being around one another. Often, relationship building happens in the small moments, not during the canned activities: I get to know my students through quick check-ins before class, through reading their papers and witnessing how their minds work, through noticing the ways they communicate with their peers. Relationship building is slow and deliberate and can't be rushed.

Caring also means looking at our students and their lives with clear eyes. Having a strengths-based view of our students doesn't mean ignoring challenges or hardships. I had a student, Gracie, who was in my class at the therapeutic school. Gracie lived with a large family in rural poverty. She had been diagnosed with a learning disability and struggled with social interactions. Seeing Gracie clearly meant understanding these conditions, not just how they impacted her but how they fit into the bigger picture. For example, I needed to understand rural poverty in my state and what the associated challenges might mean for Gracie and her family. One thing I learned from getting to know families at my school was how the lack of public transportation was a huge barrier to school involvement. Seeing this clearly helped me understand why Gracie's parents might not show up to school events, which enabled me to build bridges by providing practical alternatives, such as sending gas cards purchased by the school to offset the cost of travel, or coordinating with Gracie's mom to schedule school meetings on days when she had other errands in town. Instead of a deficit view, assuming Gracie's family didn't care about school, getting to know them and seeing them clearly helped us connect.

In addition to understanding the challenges facing Gracie, I also needed to see her strengths and assets and know what mattered to her. She loved animals. She was fiercely loyal to her friends and family. She was incredibly optimistic and always found a way to see the silver lining. To hold unconditional positive regard for Gracie, I got to know her and truly care about her, not just in the moments where these strengths shone through but also in the moments where she struggled.

Caring for all our students requires that we as teachers make a choice. Choosing unconditional positive regard is more than implementing a relationship-building strategy. It's a way of carrying ourselves that reflects our core beliefs that caring and community are the heart of education. Choosing unconditional positive regard is also an act of resistance against a system that can be dehumanizing for our students, especially students of color. In the conclusion to *Troublemakers: Lessons in Freedom From Young People at School* (2017), Carla Shalaby calls for teachers to "be love" as a way of engaging in the struggle for freedom in public life. She wrote that public love is "fierce, powerful, political, insistent" (p. 172). When we care unconditionally about our students, we fight back against a system that tries to tell these same students that they are only as worthy as their scores on a test, their acceptance into college, or their eventual income.

Choosing unconditional positive regard for Gracie meant firmly planting myself on her side, holding hope for her and her future, and refusing to buy into deficit narratives about whether or not she was worthy of care. In practice, this looked like building a strong relationship with her and, if we had a conflict, using restorative practices to make it right. It looked like reframing her challenges to other adults who worked with her when they made vague statements like, "Well, you know her family." It looked like working to unpack my own assumptions about trauma and poverty so I could see her clearly. And it also meant holding unconditional positive regard for all of my other students, because we can't pick and choose which kids deserve our care.

When children experience trauma, they are made to feel powerless, less than, unimportant, disposable. Unconditional positive regard refuses to play into trauma's false narrative. In committing to unconditional positive regard and choosing to care for our students, we build the foundation for students to thrive.

Sustaining Unconditional Positive Regard

Grounding myself in unconditional positive regard helps me build equity-centered trauma-informed relationships, but it also helps me maintain them. Working with trauma-affected students can sometimes be frustrating. Some of the coping mechanisms and relational habits that children develop as a natural response to trauma can feel confusing or challenging to us as teachers. For example, some trauma-affected children mistrust adults and authority figures by default. This is for good reason: harm to children is most often caused by adults or the lack of intervention by adults. Being careful about who to trust is a necessary survival skill. Even though intellectually I understand that, it's difficult in the moment when my attempts to connect with a student are shut down over and over again. I remember one student telling me, "You're only here for the money." While I wanted to laugh, given the reality of my paycheck, I also felt frustrated and sad: why couldn't she see that I genuinely cared and wanted to help?

Other trauma-affected students seem to trust adults too easily, crossing boundaries in ways that feel jarring. I remember meeting a new student, Leah, at the therapeutic school and settling in with her for our first class together. Usually during a first class session with new students I would offer a variety of activities, like playing a card game, taking a walk, or browsing books in the library, so I could get to know them in a low-stakes way. Most students were fairly quiet during a first meeting, answering only specific questions and generally keeping their guard up. With Leah, things were different from the first minute. She was bubbly and talkative. It felt easy to get into a conversation, and I was enjoying our time together. But as the hour went on, Leah began to share details about her life that seemed really personal. Before too long, she was near tears recounting instances of abuse and violence she had experienced. I now know that this type of oversharing is connected to what's called "indiscriminate proximity seeking," in which youth seem to attach to others too easily due to their trauma (Craig, 2017). At the time it just felt confusing and overwhelming. Building strong relationships with children and adolescents, regardless of trauma history, can be a roller coaster.

Another area that can make it hard to sustain our trauma-informed practices in relationships is our ability to notice growth. Progress, both academic and relational, for trauma-affected students can be hard to notice if you're not focusing on the small things. Unlike what you've seen in movies, healing from trauma doesn't look like one good cry session or inspirational speech and then bam, your trauma is healed forever. Trauma recovery is rarely linear.

All this combined means that it can be challenging for teachers to maintain our unconditional positive regard over the course of a relationship with a trauma-affected student. I remember working with Julia, a student at the therapeutic school who spent our class session each week with her head down on the table and her headphones in. She never engaged with me except to sometimes call me a four-letter word I can't type here. Needless to say, we didn't get much academic work done. I kept showing up, though. I held on to my unconditional positive regard like a life raft, trying to remind myself that each class session was a new day and that developing trust takes time.

I did this in a few concrete ways. First, I made use of my regularly scheduled reflective supervision meetings with our school director, Katie. The purpose of these meetings was for staff to explore how they were experiencing our work and gain valuable coaching and an outside perspective. In these meetings I was able to share my feelings, like "I must be a terrible teacher," and my questions, like "how the heck am I ever going to get through to her?" Katie's coaching helped me see the bigger picture for this student. She reassured me that even though Julia and I were missing instructional time in that moment, we would make up for it in leaps and bounds once we built a trusting relationship. Katie also validated my worries and fears, which made me feel safe enough to continue trying and let go of being perfect.

Another way I cultivated my unconditional positive regard was by intentionally choosing to see Julia's strengths. I sought out other teachers who had good relationships with her and asked for their advice. I learned about some of Julia's previous accomplishments at school, especially her talent as an artist. I also learned about her sense of humor and her dedication to her friends. As she slowly let me in, I also learned more about the challenges Julia faced. Rather than using these challenges as fuel for my pity, I chose to see Julia as a resilient person for her persistence in the face of these challenges. I began to appreciate more deeply the fact that she even showed up to school each day.

Finally, I made a point to connect with her outside of class. Even if she wasn't that interested in talking to me, I made sure to say hi regularly in the lunch line and the hall. I didn't push her to talk to me if she didn't want to, but I found that she was more open to chitchat with me while we were scraping lunch trays than when an academic task was standing between us.

So by the end of the semester, you can imagine my delight when Julia had days when the headphones stayed in but her head also stayed up and she shot quick glances over at the books and papers on the table. Sometime after that, she might even scooch her chair closer to start looking at the materials I brought. And you bet I wanted to throw a party the first time she picked up a pencil and got to work. These were small wins that I might not have noticed if I were simply looking for a grand narrative of "Troubled Student Overcomes Trauma."

Celebrating Julia's growth wouldn't have been possible if I gave up on her after the first couple of times she swore at me and put her head down. If I wrote her off as lazy, disrespectful, or unmotivated, I would have likely confirmed what she expected me to think of her. If I disciplined her, I would have been disciplining her trauma, because the walls she put up were there to keep her safe. Because I actively chose to cultivate unconditional positive regard, however, we were able to develop an authentic relationship.

When we are committed to unconditional positive regard, giving up on a student is not an option. If I treat all students with unconditional positive regard, I do not offer acceptance only to those students who have certain resources, accomplish certain tasks, or come from certain backgrounds.

I can use unconditional positive regard to check myself and my bias. If I am frustrated with a student, I remind myself, "This student has value. This student doesn't need to prove that to me." When I believe in unconditional positive regard, I dispense of the notion that to earn my respect, they need to give me respect. Respect for my students isn't transactional; it's unconditional.

For some trauma-affected students, unconditional positive regard is especially powerful in disrupting narratives about their self-concept. Trauma can profoundly damage our sense of self. Children who are abused, for example, can develop the belief that they are at fault for their own abuse. This self-blame becomes a "malignant sense of inner badness" (Herman, 1992/2015, p. 105). When we as teachers intentionally or unintentionally communicate that kids are only as good as their achievements, we can end up reinforcing that feeling of unworthiness. Unconditional acceptance can help students internalize their inherent worth and goodness.

Careful, though: don't assume that students who experience trauma are unloved or lack unconditional acceptance at home. As teachers we are poised to become powerful agents of healing through our presence as caring, responsive people in our students' lives. But we can't do that if we pity our students and their families or adopt a savior mentality. Unconditional positive regard is not pity, because it requires that we see students as wanting what they want and feeling what they feel, as their own people, not as tools for our own self-gratification. It's not about how great I am as a teacher; it's about how great we can be as a community.

ACTION STEPS

Cultivating your unconditional positive regard is a mindset shift and also takes practice and concrete changes. Here are a few ideas for building unconditional relationships:

Develop Your Lens

- I gain motivation and perspective when I read books that push my thinking about education from a philosophical standpoint, rather than the strategy-focused books I often read that are more connected to daily practice. Grounding your daily interactions in your education philosophy can help you navigate through uncertain times. A couple of my favorites that will give you some food for thought on relationships and building cultures of caring in school: *Educating Moral People* (2002) by Nel Noddings, and *Troublemakers: Lessons in Freedom from Young People at School* (2017) by Carla Shalaby. As you read and reflect on your philosophy, consider writing a personal mission statement and keeping it on display in your workspace.
- To maintain unconditional positive regard, it helps to have a colleague to give you perspective, like I had with my supervisor Katie. These perspective-keeping conversations work best with someone you trust to validate your emotions while also holding you accountable to doing your best work. Who's your Katie? It might be your supervisor, a school counselor, or a fellow

teacher. Whoever it is, make sure you invest time in these critical conversations.

Transform Your Classroom

- One of the core statements of unconditional positive regard is communicating clearly to your students, "You have value." Find ways in your classroom to recognize and celebrate each student's value. This can be as simple as rotating classroom jobs or students taking turns to facilitate advisory circles. One of my friends shared a story of students in her advisory group inventing a holiday for their classmate, just because they wanted to celebrate her. They made posters and brought in their peer's favorite snacks. Create a community environment where spontaneous celebrations of care are normal and encouraged.

Shift the Systems

- How does your school communicate unconditional positive regard for all of your students, collectively? Some schools unintentionally communicate conditional acceptance when they have awards nights only for sports teams, for example, or when a focus on grades overtakes a focus on students as whole people. Consider evaluating your school's approach to recognitions and awards through an unconditional lens: how are we intentionally or unintentionally communicating our value for each student?

8 | Make Connections, Respect Boundaries

Many teachers are concerned that trauma-informed practices mean that teachers are expected to become therapists and get too involved in the lives of their students. Other teachers are enthusiastic about the perceived permission to connect in deeper ways with students. They see trauma-informed practices as giving them the freedom to dive into discussions of the hardest parts of life together. Boundaries are a tricky business. What is the right level of involvement? How do we know when we're keeping students' social and emotional lives too distant, and how do we know when we've gotten too close?

Often teachers can drift too far in one direction: either we see ourselves as responsible only for academics and dismiss any role we can play in a student's social-emotional development, or we enmesh ourselves way too closely with students and take on a savior role. Neither is particularly helpful, and both can be harmful.

There's no exact rule that will work for everyone, so we need to be reflective and mindful in finding the appropriate boundary within our own context and setting, but we also must remember that clear boundaries and roles are nonnegotiable in creating a trauma-informed environment (Elliott et al., 2005). In this chapter I offer a few guidelines I find helpful as I consider building relationships with equity and trauma in mind. Here are the three that I revisit most often:

- Don't be a trauma detective
- Don't be the "only one"
- Be a connection maker

Don't Be a Trauma Detective

At the therapeutic school I cotaught a small group class with my coworker Mike. One of our students was Elaine, a 12-year-old girl who was bright and bubbly at times and angry and sullen at others. After class each week Mike and I would debrief to reflect on how class had gone. Through this reflection we noticed a couple of patterns with Elaine. First, she seemed to be more consistent in her interactions with me, while her relationship with Mike seemed volatile. She seemed to try to impress him at some moments and was explosively angry at him in others. Second, we observed that on some Fridays Elaine struggled way more than she did during the rest of her days at school, but not every Friday, which we found odd. We wanted to know more about Elaine in the hope we could serve her better.

Because we were in a therapeutic school setting, we had access to consultation with Elaine's school social worker. Through our consultation, we learned that Elaine had a difficult relationship with her father. We also learned that Elaine spent every other weekend at her father's house. It all seemed to make sense: she must have been struggling with Mike because he reminded her of her father, and the seemingly random Fridays must be the days before visits to her dad's house. Now that we knew what was going on, couldn't we be better teachers for Elaine?

I hear from teachers all the time that to serve trauma-affected students they need to know more. Teachers want to know the experiences and challenges of our students in the hope that this information will unlock the key to reaching and supporting them. I empathize with this desire because I've been there, as I was with Elaine. The truth is, however, that it's not necessary to know all the details of students' traumatic experiences to support them in a trauma-informed way. In fact, sometimes the desire to know what's *really* going on can distract us from being helpful, and pushing for details can actually be harmful.

No one owes anyone else the details of their trauma, and it can be exploitative to require this of students.

In the case of me, Mike, and Elaine, for example, it did feel helpful to know what was going on. But the problem was that neither Mike nor I were trained mental health clinicians, and even if we were, we weren't *Elaine's* mental health clinicians—we were her teachers. Outside the context of a clinical relationship, the conclusions we made about Elaine's challenges were simply assumptions, and these assumptions weren't particularly helpful. If we assumed that Elaine's problem with Mike was just a manifestation of her challenges with her dad, it might let Mike off the hook of building or repairing his relationship with her. If I assumed that the problem on Fridays was about visiting dad's house, it could obfuscate a problem with my class planning, like a lack of structure or even my own end-of-week jitters rubbing off on my students.

There may be times when it is helpful for students to share details of their challenges, or when a family chooses to share a trigger for staff to watch out for. In Elaine's case, her social worker communicated details to us as a part of Elaine's overall therapeutic plan. In any school, disclosures about students' personal lives and challenges must be led by the student and family/caregivers, often in consultation with mental health professionals. Teachers should treat any information with care and confidentiality. Far too often, I have heard teachers treat the traumatic experiences of students like gossip, especially in smaller communities. It's normal to want to talk about student experiences, but there is a difference between finding time to process and sharing stories for shock value.

Even if individual teachers aren't asking students directly to share their stories of trauma, schools often require these stories in order for students to get support. Students living in poverty are often asked to apply for assistance again and again throughout the school year, each time their families cannot afford a resource, a field trip, hot lunch, or a sports fee—"performing their poverty" in order to access their education (Gorski, 2018). Consider the typical structure of American special education, in which students must be diagnosed and demonstrate deficiency in order to access needed resources and support for learning. Does your school require these same types of disclosures or performances for students to receive social, emotional, and mental health support?

In a perfect world no shame or stigma would be connected to poverty, disability, or trauma, but that's not the world we live in. Required sharing of hardships can cause humiliation and shame and can create great mistrust between students and their families and school. Recall the discussion in Part II about a universal approach. Now recall that the class Mike and I cotaught was with a whole group of students, not just Elaine. Instead of zeroing in on the challenges with Elaine and Mike, we could instead focus our energy on creating systems for the whole class that supported relationship building and working through times of stress. Even though we might have focused on Elaine's struggles, she certainly wasn't the only one in class who sometimes snapped at Mike or who had a hard time on Fridays. We could help Elaine by helping the whole class, using the proactive priorities like predictability and connection to guide our work.

It's not our job as teachers to be trauma detectives (Venet, 2019b). We can do trauma-informed work without directly engaging students in dialogue about their trauma or being privy to all of the details of their pain. To maintain healthy boundaries in our student-teacher relationships, we must honor and respect our students' privacy and, when necessary, share information only with great intention and care. If there are reasons for students to share specific information, such as a trigger that is present in the school environment, a student, their family, and any mental health practitioners or medical professionals should make those decisions in collaboration with school. Students should always be in control of how and when their story is shared.

School leaders can help prevent trauma detective work by assessing communication structures within the school to make sure that teachers understand when, how, and why they should share (or not share) student information. I encourage leaders to be transparent in their decision making in this area. Otherwise, schools may develop a culture where teachers assume they are being left out of the loop. Teachers feel that they should know the details of what's going on, but leaders can reframe this by focusing on what the student needs, not what the student is specifically experiencing.

Here's an example of how a school leader might communicate with a student's teachers while respecting confidentiality:

> *Hi, Mohamed's teachers. I wanted to let you know that Mohamed has been having a hard couple of weeks, and you might notice that in your classes. In talking with Mohamed, he wanted me to share that he acknowledges he's not caught up right now and thanks you for your patience. He would like to keep the details to himself, but he appreciates when you ask him how he's doing or simply take a moment to ask him about his dogs or how the basketball team is doing. Please know that Mohamed is already connected to support through the counseling office. If you have any questions about supporting Mohamed, you can reach out to his counselor, Ms. Wright.*

Don't Be the "Only One"

Boundaries are complicated. On one hand, we shouldn't mindlessly share details about our students. But we also need to pay attention to the other end of the spectrum: as teachers, we can't keep secrets with students, or put ourselves in a position where we become the "only one" a student can turn to.

When we build strong relationships with students, sometimes they trust us enough to share their worries, fears, and hardships. Teachers can become trusted witnesses of students' lives, but we need to be mindful when there are signs that students need more support. If I'm operating from a savior mentality, it feels good when a student says "you're the only cool teacher," "you're the only one I like here," or "you're the only one I can tell." If I'm operating from a connection-focused, unconditional mindset, I might instead be troubled by these statements. Children need many more relationships in their lives than just one trusted teacher. If I hear "you're the only one I can trust," it might be a sign that I can put more energy into being a connection maker (more on that in a moment).

Remember how I said that boundaries are complicated? For students whose identities are marginalized within the school community, a teacher who shares an identity with these students may truly represent the only safe relationship in school. For example, young people may not be able to safely talk about exploring their gender identity with their parents and turn instead to an openly transgender teacher. The few Black students in a mostly white school may be able to connect with the only Black teacher in ways that don't feel safe with the white teachers. Our identities and the ways these interact with our students' identities inform our boundaries.

In any of these scenarios, teachers still need to consider the potential dangers of being the "only one," especially when it comes to keeping secrets, privacy, and the confidences of our students. We shouldn't hold any information secret with or about a student, or ask students to keep secrets for us, because secrecy can replicate unhealthy and traumatic dynamics (Romero et al., 2018). Abused children are often threatened or coerced into staying quiet. Some children fear violence and other dangerous repercussions if they were to disclose the abuse (Herman, 1992/2015). If and when our students disclose that they are experiencing abuse or other trauma, we need to be responsive. In most states, teachers are mandated reporters, meaning that we are required to contact state children's services if we suspect that child abuse or neglect has taken place (Child Welfare Information Gateway, 2019, p. 68). This requirement means that we cannot legally keep secrets about children's trauma.

Teachers and school leaders sometimes find themselves in positions of breaking trust with children and families when they are required to make a report after promising that information would be held in confidence. It is better instead to build trust by being clear ahead of time about our role. When we establish relationships with students and families, we should be clear about the difference between confidential information and secrets and be up front about the times when we would share information. For example, if a student comes to see me during lunch and says, "If I tell you something, will you promise to keep it between us?" It can feel difficult at that moment to set a boundary and explain, "No, I'm sorry, I can't. Let me tell you why." But it's harmful if I instead said, "Of course, you can trust me," and then later needed to break that trust by following through on mandated reporting. Applying the proactive priority of predictability (Chapter 5), we build predictability when students and families know what to expect and trust that we will follow through. Being clear about communication helps create trust.

Beyond the specific issue of abuse disclosure, teachers need to pay attention to the nature of our closer relationships with students. Even if we are mindful of the dynamics around information sharing, we still should not cultivate relationships that place too much weight on a single teacher-student relationship. Consider this: in most schools, students end their relationship with their teachers at the end of the school year. Some students may stay connected voluntarily, or say hi in the hallways, but our day-to-day role in their lives comes to a close. While I do think that schools should restructure so that students and teachers have more multiyear relationships, we should also consider what this time limit means for our relationships with students.

If we see ourselves in a savior role, then we are rushed to do as much "healing" as we possibly can within the time constraint of our year with students. At the end of the year we might feel failure and loss when students haven't made the growth that we wanted or expected. If we see ourselves as connection makers, rather than being "the one," we see our role as helping increase the number and quality of relationships in each student's life.

Be a Connection Maker

The role of a trauma-informed teacher should primarily be that of a connection builder (Venet, 2019b). Because we know that relationships are so important to address trauma and buffer its effects, as teachers we can position ourselves as facilitators of those relationships. This means not only building our own relationships with students but also facilitating relationship building between students and serving as a bridge to other caring adults and resources.

There is a common saying that just one caring adult can change the trajectory of the life of a child. This is true: research says that the presence of caring adults is an essential factor in youth resilience (Masten, 2018). As teachers, however, we shouldn't take this to mean that we are the *only* caring adult in a student's life. As a connection maker, my goal is to increase the number and quality of relationships, recognizing that my students already have valuable relationships in their lives.

Being a connection maker can look like fostering relationships among our students. Even in schools where students know one another well, we can help students deepen their skills. We can incorporate lessons or activities that explore what it means to be a good friend, how to disagree respectfully, or how to advocate for a peer. We can intentionally use meaningful academic projects in the form of group work to build relationships, especially when we support those groups to do higher-order collaboration rather than just dividing up tasks or taking turns. As education philosopher Nel Noddings has explained, "Students should be encouraged to work together, to help one another— not just to improve academic performance, but to gain competence in caring" (2002, p. 20). Being a part of a caring community requires that we practice things like compromise, reflective listening, and collaboration. The best SEL happens not in 10-minute add-on lessons but in the opportunities we create for authentic practice and reflection on that practice.

Connection making also looks like helping students build connections with their communities both within and outside of school. For example, my colleague Christie's students started a Students Organizing Against Racism group, part of the national organization Courageous Conversations about Race, that helps students learn how to disrupt hate speech in their peer groups and to advocate for policy changes in their school by presenting at school board meetings. Connections like these help students see themselves as the valuable members of the community that they are. For students who have been marginalized and told that their voices do not matter, this is also a way to help them take an active role (Chapter 13 explores student advocacy in more depth).

Community connections can also be powerful for students to find identity-affirming spaces. Sometimes school isn't a safe place to explore gender identity, for example. There may not be enough students sharing a common religious, cultural, or ethnic background to start a school-based student group based on that shared identity. Connection-making teachers can support students by identifying local community-based opportunities for connection, like introducing a student to a queer youth center's drop-in support group or sharing the link to an online community forum for Muslim girls interested in engineering. We should make these connections at the same time as we also work to create affirming spaces within our schools, recognizing that it shouldn't be an either/or choice: students should feel included and supported in the school *and* in the community.

Finally, connection making means that we look to connect our students to the right people and resources for support, being humble that this might not be us. This is connected to how we maintain boundaries. If a student comes to me and wants to deeply process a traumatic experience, I need to be able to recognize that doing so may not fit within my role as a teacher, and compassionately connect her to a person or organization that is more equipped to do so. I can do this only if I know who and what those resources are and how to help my students access them. Here's how I might make this redirection for a student:

> Thank you so much for feeling comfortable to talk to me. I can hear how much this is upsetting you and how you need to talk about it. I want to let you know that I care about you and want to help you, but I think you might benefit from talking to someone who has more perspective on this than I do. Have you ever met our school counselor Kate? She plays Dungeons and Dragons like you do. Want to walk over together five minutes before the end of lunch and I can introduce you?

In this example, I validate the trust the student showed in me and reaffirm our connection. I then offer a connection to a resource, explaining why this might benefit the student, and find a personal connection to help ease any anxiety or fear that the student might have about talking to someone new. Importantly, I end with making a plan to help the student access the resource, ensuring that I follow through so that the student's concern doesn't get lost in the shuffle because of my redirection. If the resource isn't a person within our school, I might pull up the appropriate website or phone number with my student and help make the first call or send the initial email, or help the student write out a script to do it alone. When doing this type of bridging, we also should be careful not to imply that we are pushing a student away or passing them off. If we have genuine and caring relationships with our students, we instead communicate that we're looking to enhance their network of support.

Seeing ourselves as connection makers supports an equity stance because it requires that we look at the opportunities for relationships in our students' lives, as well as the barriers. Mathew Portell, principal of an elementary school in Nashville, Tennessee, that implemented trauma-informed practices, once told me he and his staff are "barrier warriors, knocking down barriers like it's our job." Indeed, removing barriers *is* our job as educators. Our students, like all of us, deserve to have lives filled with rich and varied relationships. As connection builders and barrier warriors, we can help them build those relationships.

Because boundaries are complicated, our ongoing reflection is required. Here are some reflection questions to help you as you consider how to build and maintain boundaries that work for you, in your context, with your students:

- When it comes to talking about emotions and life experiences, what's safe and authentic for my role as an educator? What feels safe and enjoyable to share with my students, and for my students to share with me? What feels like it crosses a line?
- How aligned am I with my coworkers when it comes to boundaries? If we are not aligned, how might that feel to students? How could I start a conversation with my colleagues about this?
- Who are the other support people in my students' lives? Do I or other teachers have connections with these people? How might we collaborate in support of our students?
- How might I help my students strengthen their relationships with others?
- Who/what are the resources in our community for student support? Do I know enough about these to empathetically redirect students? How can students access this information on their own?
- What sets off my internal alarm when it comes to boundaries? What are my own triggers or challenges?
- Who can I go to for support and consultation?

Mind the Gap

My journey with my student Julia (see Chapter 7), spending an entire semester building trust, was one experience with one student in a small school where I was given the gift of time. For most teachers, there isn't just one Julia but many students in each of our classes who need more intentional relationship building and whose trust isn't easily won. This comes back to the tension I have described between doing the work now toward equity-centered trauma-informed schools and recognizing how many systems need to change. Most schools are not conducive to building deep relationships or to following students' lead about the pace of learning.

As teachers who care deeply about our students, it's distressing to see the gap between what our students need and what schools actually provide. It can be tempting to try to fill the gap by spending all of our evenings and weekends providing personalized feedback, or paying out of our pocket for the things our students need, or blurring boundaries as we attempt to be a parent, coach, therapist, teacher, and friend all in one. But we cannot try to make up for all of the deficiencies of the school system by sacrificing ourselves for the cause. Chris Lehmann and Zac Chase, educators and authors of *Building School 2.0* (2015), wrote about the dangers of savior mentality in this tough-love note to teachers:

> *You are not the savior of students. You are not the one they have been waiting for. No prophecy has foretold your coming. You are a person of passion and training who is working to help other people learn. That is good, and that should be enough. You are helping. You are the shoulder on which to cry. You are the one who connects your students with the resources they desperately need. You will not be the one who "saves" them. To suggest as much robs students of their resiliency and agency. (p. 269)*

Becoming a savior or a martyr not only is a recipe for burnout but also does a disservice to our students. As Lehmann and Chase wrote, what you can do in your role as a teacher needs to be enough. They go on to say that if teaching "costs you everything, it's costing you too much" (p. 270).

ACTION STEPS

Establishing and maintaining boundaries isn't a one-and-done task. Most teachers build dozens to hundreds of new relationships each year, which means we have many opportunities to hone our relationship skills. These action steps can help us become better connection makers:

Develop Your Lens

- Use the reflection questions from this chapter to think about your own boundaries. In addition to the questions on the list, imagine yourself as a student in your classroom or school. Would your own personal boundaries be respected? What would it feel like to share the information or experiences that your students are asked to share? This thought exercise can give insight into how you then adjust your stance around information-sharing and boundaries in your own work.

Transform Your Classroom

- Think about your curriculum in your role of connection maker. What is the balance of individual work and group work? When are students producing work just for the audience of you or their classmates, and when are students presenting their learning in the community? How might students collaborate with those outside of the school building to enrich their learning?
- Plan a lesson or write an informational sheet for your students about confidentiality and communication based on your students' age, your role, and your school's policies. What do your students need to know about boundaries in your classroom? When might you present this information? Are there points in the year where you could refresh and revisit these guidelines? If you already teach concepts like digital citizenship or social skills,

you can incorporate confidentiality and boundaries into these topics.

Shift the Systems

- Consider creating a policy that describes how and when confidential information is shared among staff. Try to answer questions like these:

  - When and why is confidential information related to learning shared (IEP-related information, grades, learning progress, etc.)?
  - When and why is confidential information related to physical and mental health shared (Allergies, diagnoses, mental health concerns, etc.)?
  - In what situations are teachers encouraged or required to share information that students or families tell them?
  - To what degree do you involve students and families in decisions about information sharing? How can they review and participate in this process?

Part IV

Shift 3: Move From Mindset to Systems Change

Marta, a high school sophomore, lived in a chaotic household. Adults who were supposed to take care of her were instead putting her in harm's way, leaving Marta to try to cope with the danger and confusion while also attending school every day. One of Marta's coping strategies was to smoke marijuana. At school Marta was caught with marijuana twice. She received a warning and then a one-day suspension because of the school's automatic and nonnegotiable substance use policy.

Sometime after this suspension the school became aware of Marta's situation at home. School staff leapt into action to support her. Her special education case manager, Jasmine, focused on building a supportive relationship with Marta to help her feel safe at school, while others dealt with coordination of social service agencies who could step in to remove the dangerous person from Marta's home.

It was difficult work for the adults, and in the meantime, Marta continued to struggle to feel safe either at home or at school. Eventually, it seemed like the team's efforts were paying off, and Marta was finally getting into a routine at school: checking in with safe adults like Jasmine, attending all of her classes. But then Marta came to school high again. She was suspended for a week because of the automatic and nonnegotiable school policy.

The individual teachers and staff who had supported Marta were trauma-informed. The school policy was not. In an instant, Jasmine and her colleagues watched all of the work of the team undone, as a scared teen girl was told she wasn't welcome in the school because of the coping strategy she used in the face of overwhelming circumstances.

When I say that trauma-informed practices are a mindset shift, I don't mean that the work happens only in the minds and hearts of educators. Equity-centered trauma-informed practice requires that systems, rules, and procedures undergo tangible change. We literally need to rethink and rewrite policies and procedures.

Schools and school districts are often large and complex systems, and policies written for these systems have to meet a variety of needs: legal requirements, educational best practice, and the needs of caregivers, school staff, and students. Writing an effective policy is not easy, but as we can see from Marta's experience, it is extremely important.

What if Marta's school had a more flexible substance use policy? What if Jasmine and the rest of the teacher team were able to collaborate with Marta and school administrators to determine a path forward that was both fair and caring? Schools, of course, need to have ways to address substance use among students. But a trauma-informed environment recognizes that substance use may be one coping strategy that students use to survive. We can't be in the business of punishing a student for trying to survive.

A teacher's mindset shift matters, but recall Principle 3 of equity-centered trauma-informed education: *trauma-informed education as a full ecosystem*. This means that changes at the classroom level need to rely on changes at the policy level, and vice versa, for either to function. Our practices are interconnected with policy and procedure.

I often work with teachers like Jasmine, the caring special education teacher. These teachers participate in professional learning about trauma-informed practices, cultivate their own mindset shift, and transform their classrooms. Sometimes they implement strategies like calming corners or teaching mindful breathing. They might adjust their curriculum with flexibility and empowerment in mind. These teachers move from trauma awareness to trauma-informed action in their spheres of influence, but then they hit a wall, as when Jasmine's efforts were undermined by the immovable school substance use policy. Despite their best efforts, school-wide policy does not always have the best interests of their trauma-affected students at heart. The most trauma-informed classroom teachers still cannot create a fully equity-centered trauma-informed environment if school policy harms kids. Transformational teachers are limited when we allow inequitable school policy and practice to stand.

The frustration of stalled progress gives way to blame: teachers complain that principals aren't willing to make necessary changes, principals say the same about superintendents and district leadership, and district leadership frets about conflict-prone school boards. These school politics are real, as is the pressure from state and federal education regulations. Yet these difficulties do not excuse us from digging into the hard work of policy change. As long as we leave policies in place that perpetuate inequity and create traumatic situations for students, we can't call ourselves trauma-informed.

Part IV explores the third shift, from trauma-informed practices as the responsibility of individual teachers to *trauma-informed education as embedded in the way that we do school, from policies to practice*. Trauma-informed teachers need trauma-informed leaders. For trauma-informed practices to fully change the entire ecosystem of a school, they need to be implemented at all levels and supported by all school staff, from dedicated teachers to strong leaders to engaged support staff.

This shift moves us toward:

- **Principle 3: Systems oriented**—Trauma-informed education is a full ecosystem, not a list of strategies.
- **Principle 4: Human centered**—Trauma-informed education means centering our shared humanity.

Chapters 9 and 10 directly address school leaders who have influence over policy and who supervise teachers. Chapter 9 focuses on teacher wellness and how administrators can create communities of care and personalized support for educators. In Chapter 10, I highlight how to prioritize equity-centered trauma-informed practices in professional development so that teachers can make sustainable growth over time. Chapter 11 explores how to create equity-centered trauma-informed policies that can create lasting systems change in schools. Because all three chapters concern systems change and leadership, instead of the action steps in three areas that I've included in other chapters, here I provide action steps connected to "leading peers and leading up." These action steps are for those who don't consider themselves leaders or don't hold a leadership title, with suggestions and resources for creating systems change from your role.

9 | Support Teacher Wellness

Teachers are people, and many of us have experienced trauma. Supporting trauma-affected children while you manage your own trauma is incredibly difficult, yet this is the day-to-day experience of many educators. In the same way that authoritarian teaching practices can be triggering for trauma-affected students, authoritarian leadership styles can be triggering for adults in the workplace. Leaders can change school culture by modeling the unconditional care and equity-centered practices that you hope your teachers will use with their students.

When we feel depleted, it's hard to care for others. Most teachers know the feeling all too well: we come to school and put on a smiling face for our students, while inside we struggle with heartbreak, worry, or fear. When teachers struggle with their own trauma, it can feel impossible to be responsive to the trauma of our students and our school community.

It's even harder to do equity-centered trauma-informed work when we don't feel cared about as people. Teaching is already a hard job, and we struggle to do it well when there's added stress, whether from dehumanizing leadership practices from administrators, microaggressions from colleagues, or simply trying to survive in a toxic work environment.

Teacher wellness is an equity issue. Teacher burnout lowers student motivation and worsens student stress (Lever et al., 2017). When teachers feel unsupported by school leadership or work in poor conditions, they leave their schools or even the teaching profession, and this teacher turnover lowers student achievement (Curran et al., 2019). For schools to provide high-quality learning environments, we must take care of teachers.

The same way that we need to communicate our care to students for a trauma-informed environment, we need to create a culture of care for all of the adults in the school. In many books on trauma-informed education, teachers are encouraged to engage in self-care, build exercise routines, or practice mindfulness. All of those things are important. At the same time, teacher wellness is not the sole responsibility of individual teachers, and to suggest as much blames teachers for the systemic conditions in schools that cause their stress. Therefore, this chapter is addressed to school leaders, focusing on what they must do to create a positive and supportive work environment for their teachers.

Creating a Culture of Care

Most of my recommendations for leaders to develop a culture of care for their teachers are found by turning back to Chapters 6 and 7 and replacing the word "student" with "staff member." One piece from those chapters of particular interest for leaders is the ethic of care. I wrote about Nel Noddings and her distinction between caring *about* and caring *for*. In a community based on an ethic of care, we care for one another, not just for our students. The ethic of care is connected to the principle of humanization. Remember, humanization is the foundation for equity-centered trauma-informed practice. An ethic of care attends to the needs of teachers, staff, and students as people.

Creating a culture of care requires attention and dedication. Principal Chris Lehmann of Science Leadership Academy in Philadelphia wrote about sustaining an ethic of care at his school: "We cannot simply just say 'we care for one another' without putting in the hard work of thinking about what that means" (2016, n.p.). Lehmann shares that in his school sustaining the ethic of care looks like frequent conversations, especially in student advisory groups. For example, when the school culture felt in need of a reset, advisory groups discussed such questions as, "How should we show our care for students with unpopular opinions?" and "What's the best way to let each other know when sarcasm goes from funny to mean?" These conversations involved the students and the adults together because the school understands all of its members to be in community together.

I remember similar conversations from my time as both a teacher and a leader at the therapeutic school. Our school director, Katie (you may remember her from her wise mentorship in Chapter 7) regularly facilitated conversations among our staff to intentionally address staff culture. She had one version of this where she taped a line on the floor, labeling one end "belongs in our staff culture" and the other end "doesn't belong in our staff culture." After reviewing our mission statement, she handed out cards with scenarios: "Teachers collaborate on lesson planning," "Teachers go out to the bar after work on Friday," and "Teachers interrupt one another's classes for quick questions" were a few. For each scenario, we discussed as a group how that might fit in or not fit into our staff culture and placed the cards along the line. For example, our school was under the umbrella of a nonprofit that focused on supporting youth substance use recovery. In our conversation, we talked about how some staff might choose to work there because of their own commitment to substance use recovery, and how it might feel to those staff if all social events took place at our local bar. Importantly, Katie wasn't mandating anything one way or another or suggesting that teachers weren't allowed to socialize outside of work. Instead, she created the space for us to consider how we wanted to live up to our shared values. We recognized that a healthy and caring work environment for the adults translated into a healthy and caring workplace for the kids.

As leaders, we have to dedicate time and energy to sustaining an ethic of care. Care for all the humans in your school should be a driving force behind decision making. An ethic of care, like Carla Shalaby's (2017) concept of "public love," is political. By choosing to center care for your staff and your students, you are consciously choosing an alternative in a school system that often prioritizes achievement and testing above human well-being. Being a caring leader is a powerful stance. As Noddings wrote, "There is nothing mushy about caring. It is the strong, resilient backbone of human life" (2002, p. 101).

Of course, a caring school culture on its own isn't enough to ensure equity or a trauma-informed environment. But equity-centered trauma-informed schools require a culture of care to be sustainable. School change can be challenging and messy, and conflict can come up. It's uncomfortable to confront oppression and the ways we perpetuate it as teachers. To provide an environment where students can be fully human, we have to create that same permission for all of the adults in the school.

Helping the Helpers

Creating a culture of care is a proactive way to support staff. Leaders also need to be responsive. When we engage in the emotional work of caring for our students, we also open ourselves up to the stress that comes with emotional connection. If you've ever woken up in the middle of the night worried about a student who didn't show up to school that day, or cried behind your closed classroom door after yet another student meltdown, you know this stress (you're not alone—I've done both more than once). This stress can manifest in different ways, such as burnout, compassion fatigue, and vicarious trauma (see the box on secondary traumatic stress).

Vicarious trauma isn't a sign of a bad teacher or weak person—it's a normal response to the stress that comes from caring deeply for others and witnessing their struggles. Teachers juggle many job responsibilities, including planning, facilitating, completing mountains of paperwork, attending meetings, giving meaningful feedback, designing our classrooms, communicating with parents, and attempting to build relationships with dozens or hundreds of students at once. We're held to high professional standards (sometimes without much support). Given all of this, of course we're going to be stressed at times. We shouldn't expect that simply pushing forward will somehow help us manage this stress. Instead, we need time built into our professional lives to slow down and address it.

SECONDARY TRAUMATIC STRESS: A FEW BASICS

Vicarious trauma, *secondary traumatic stress*, and *trauma exposure response* are all terms for the stress that happens when we empathetically witness the traumatic response of those we care about. It is the "emotional residue of exposure" to others' experiences of trauma (American Counseling Association, 2011). We experience vicarious trauma when we witness the pain and distress of others and have a sense of powerlessness to help. Even if you aren't talking with students directly about their traumatic experiences or providing counseling, you can still experience secondary traumatic stress.

Some of the potential signs of vicarious trauma include a preoccupation with the stories of others' trauma, disrupted sleep or appetite, and stress, anxiety, or depression. These signs overlap greatly with the signs of experiencing trauma directly, and it's possible for teachers to both directly experience trauma in school and also experience vicarious trauma. Teachers who witness violence in school, for example, or who are targets of harassment in the workplace, may experience direct traumatic stress. Our own past experiences of trauma can also be triggered when we develop secondary traumatic stress (National Child Traumatic Stress Network, 2011).

In her book *Trauma Stewardship* (2009), Laura L. van Dernoot Lipsky offers another way to think about vicarious trauma: "When we refer to trauma exposure response, we are talking about the ways in which the world looks and feels like a different place to you as a result of your doing your work" (p. 41). Lipsky identifies 16 warning signs of a trauma exposure response. You may recognize some of these signs from times when you or your colleagues have been exposed to student trauma:

- Feeling helpless and hopeless
- A sense that one can never do enough
- Hypervigilance
- Diminished creativity
- Inability to embrace complexity
- Minimizing
- Chronic exhaustion/physical ailments

- Inability to listen/deliberate avoidance
- Dissociative moments
- Sense of persecution
- Guilt
- Fear
- Anger and cynicism
- Inability to empathize/numbing
- Addictions
- Grandiosity: an inflated sense of importance related to one's work

No matter the specific nature of the stress response, teachers need support to sustain our work in a school environment impacted by trauma.

One thing leaders can do to help teachers care for themselves is to provide them with opportunities to slow down. It's hard to even notice that we're stressed if we don't have time to stop and reflect. I remember one particularly stressful winter while I was teaching at the therapeutic school. It seemed like a student crisis erupted every few days. My team was understaffed, and we didn't have substitute teachers, so no one had any down time as we covered one another's classes. I developed a rash on my arm and kept switching my laundry detergent and body wash, assuming I must be having an allergic reaction. Several months and a doctor's visit later, I finally had a lightbulb moment: I had stress hives. I hadn't taken enough time to slow down and reflect during those months to even recognize that I was stressed. My body told me instead. Sadly, I'm not alone in having this experience. I've talked to countless teachers who are so stressed that their health is significantly impacted.

Leaders must make teacher wellness a school-wide priority rather than leaving it up to individual teachers to self-care their way out of it. School conditions have a direct impact on an individual's ability to manage their stress. It's common for people-serving organizations, like schools and nonprofits, to develop an organizational culture built on scarcity and a sense of urgency. This compromises their ability to sustain the work toward their stated mission and values (Lipsky, 2009). To combat vicarious trauma in your school, one of your roles as a leader is helping teachers slow down and reflect.

Schools can support this by building in reflection and sense-making time. Some schools may dedicate a special meeting time once per month; others may leave it up to teacher teams to incorporate into their team-level meetings. At the therapeutic school, we had monthly wellness group meetings where we reflected on our well-being with peers, as well as biweekly reflective one-to-one meetings with our direct supervisor.

Reflective Supervision

Reflective supervision is a common (and often required) practice in the mental health field. It can also be a powerful practice for educators. Supervision typically meets educational, supportive, and administrative needs: education about best practices and approaches to the work, support around the employee's emotional experience and challenges, and administrative functions like keeping aligned with policies or engaging in the evaluation process (Varghese et al., 2018). This isn't just a meeting with the principal where you review a teacher's yearly observation: supervision is an ongoing, relationship-focused time set aside for the goal of supporting teachers.

One of the organizational benefits of reflective supervision is increased retention. As a teacher, I can say that reflective supervision saved me from quitting. I remember many times when I felt overwhelmed by the stress of vicarious trauma. I felt burned out and hopeless, wondering if anything I did to help my students was making a difference. Sometimes I blamed my students, convincing myself that the problem was their lack of motivation or their willful defiance. In some schools, this type of frustration can build up over months or even years, leading to simmering resentment or ultimately to teachers leaving the profession. With regularly scheduled supervision every other week and a strong relationship with my school director, there was no way for me to stew under the radar. Katie could always get me back on track through her insightful questioning, coaching, and holding me to high standards.

When I became a leader at the therapeutic school, facilitating supervision was one of my favorite parts of my job. Sometimes we sat for supervision in my office or the teacher's classroom, sometimes we'd go on walks around the neighborhood while we talked, sometimes we'd drop into the local coffee shop to have supervision after the student day ended. Supervision was most effective when it was an authentic conversation. Usually I simply started by asking, "How's it going?" and then let the conversation flow from there. Usually the conversation was unstructured, but I kept the three functions of supervision in mind—educational, support, and administrative—to make sure that by the end of our time we addressed them all.

In a typical supervision meeting of about half an hour, my teachers would often start by checking in with me about how they were doing in general, offering updates on family or hobbies or chatting about the TV show we both watched. Then we would move into "how's work going?" and teachers would often share particular highlights or struggles from the past two weeks. Often, supervision included a deep dive conversation about a particular student. These conversations are opportunities to coach teachers around implementing equity-centered trauma-informed practices. For example, one of my teachers, Tony, was frustrated with Siobhan, a tenth-grade student. Siobhan was loud, seemed to disagree with everything Tony said, and frequently derailed her classmates when she refused to participate. On our supervision walks around the neighborhood, Tony and I had the time to talk through all of the dynamics at play. There were a few loud teenage boys in his class, but it seemed he wasn't getting frustrated in the same way as with Siobhan. He was pushing Siobhan to be quiet and compliant like the other girls in his class, he realized, while Siobhan was making it clear at top volume that she needed to be heard. We brainstormed together how Tony might create more leadership opportunities for Siobhan, and I provided some resources and reading for Tony on gender equity in the classroom. Supervision was invaluable for actually making classrooms more equitable. Tony already believed that gender equity in teaching was important. Through our reflective conversations he was able to recognize where his actions weren't meeting up with those beliefs and then make changes.

Facilitating supervision effectively requires practice, skill, and boundaries. Supervision is not therapy. We can help teachers process and reflect on their work, but leaders should also be aware of the resources in our communities so we can refer teachers for additional support. In my work as a leader, I would share openly with my supervisees that I had a therapist and that this provided meaningful support in my life. Your leadership can help destigmatize mental health support and create an environment where teachers feel safe asking for help.

Whenever you make time for slowing down and reflecting, you are choosing to work against institutionalized values of our school system that prioritize rushing over deliberate action, benchmarks, and scores over relationships. It may take time to build trust with your teachers so they can be vulnerable in supervision, but in a parallel way to our work with students, all of the time investing in relationships is well worth it.

Go Beyond Cutesy Wellness

Slowing down and reflecting aren't the only ways we can support wellness in our schools. As leaders we should also think about how we can demonstrate our care and support for teachers, building a culture of community care in addition to self-care.

These demonstrations of care should be authentic and make a real impact on the working conditions of teachers. When I ask teachers about what wellness opportunities are offered at their school, I usually hear things like:

"We did a workshop on making a healthy salad-in-a-jar for lunch."

"We had a chair massage therapist come in the week before grades were due."

"The principal brought donuts to our staff meeting during Teacher Appreciation Week."

These are examples of what I call "cutesy wellness": things that seem cute and helpful but make no difference in teachers' long-term wellness or the sustainability of their jobs. As discussed in Chapter 4, wellness isn't just bubble baths and yoga. Yet this type of "cutesy" wellness is sometimes all that's offered to teachers. Any of these gestures could come across as genuine and caring if they are done in an environment where the leadership already demonstrates consistent support for her staff. If there is a general attitude of mistrust or lack of support, these gestures can feel insulting or belittling. For teachers who are up at night worrying about their students or reeling from an active-shooter drill, salad-in-a-jar isn't going to help.

As a leader, I challenge you to think beyond these surface-level strategies and think about how to help teachers actually sustain their work and take care of themselves and one another. Remember Principle 4 of equity-centered trauma-informed education, *centering our shared humanity*: how can we support teachers to be seen, valued, and supported as full people? In my experience, what teachers really need to foster their wellness is time, money, support, and autonomy.

- *Time:* Look at your school year calendar with a group of teachers and identify the days or weeks when teachers feel most stressed about their workload. Plan to cancel all nonessential meetings in the weeks leading up to paperwork deadlines or semester change-overs so teachers can reduce the amount of work they must do outside of contract hours. Also take a critical look at your agenda before every faculty meeting and cancel meetings that are mostly announcements—send an email instead.
- *Money:* The word *money* here can represent a teacher's total compensation and benefits package. Wellness is difficult to achieve if you are not making a living wage or cannot access health care. Work collaboratively with union leaders, district offices, and teachers to fight for fair pay and benefits for your staff. Make sure to include noncontract staff such as cafeteria workers, custodians, and paraprofessionals in your advocacy.
- *Support:* What do your staff need from you, and how do you know? If you haven't done so lately, gather staff feedback about the types of support they hope to receive from leaders and respond accordingly. This might look like improving lines of communication,

providing coaching, supporting parent-teacher communication, or simply spending more time listening in one-on-one check-ins. You as an individual don't need to meet teachers' every need, but be intentional about delegating and check often to assess whether teachers feel their needs are being met.

- *Autonomy:* One of the top complaints I hear from teachers is how school and district leaders micromanage their professional lives. Leaders can foster an environment of autonomy and agency among teachers by providing them with freedom to exercise their professional judgement along with resources to continually grow as educators. Simply put: trust your teachers.

Sustaining trauma-informed work should not be a question of self-care on its own. Yes, as helping professionals we are each responsible for taking care of ourselves, but we can't be expected to do it on our own. If we want to hold teachers accountable for engaging in the complex work of equity-centered trauma-informed schools, we need to give them the resources to do so. As leaders, creating a caring community among our staff needs to come first, not as an extra.

Once you create an environment in which teachers feel supported as professionals, with the necessary resources to do their job well, bring on the donuts! Cutesy wellness can feel like affirming reminders of care when it's done in the context of a healthy and positive school culture.

ACTION STEPS: LEADING PEERS AND LEADING UP

- *Offer to facilitate peer supervision.* It can be as simple as providing a space to check in about how teaching is going, or you can use a formal protocol for discussing student work. I like the protocols from the School Reform Initiative: https://www.schoolreforminitiative.org/protocols/
- *Learn more about caring organizational culture.* Teachers and school leaders alike can benefit from reading Laura L. van Dernoot Lipsky's *Trauma Stewardship: An Everyday Guide to Caring for Self While Caring for Others* (2009). Lipsky clearly illustrates

the warning signs of trauma exposure response and offers guidance for caring for ourselves. The book also contains suggestions
for leaders on how to create a caring culture within organizations.
The suggestions in Lipsky's book can help you craft feedback for
leaders on how to support teachers in managing vicarious trauma.
- *Check in.* Creating a positive staff culture can be led by principals but ultimately requires that we each express our care for our
coworkers. You can start by simply making it a point to chat with
one coworker you don't know very well each week or organizing a social outing that's open to all. Entrenched social dynamics among teaching staff can be challenging—be the change you
want to see in your colleagues!

10 Foster Professional Growth

I f you've ever been a teacher, you've probably worked at a school where you heard something like this:

> *This year, we're starting a new initiative on proficiency-based learning. This goes well with our initiative to implement social-emotional learning. Don't forget about our initiative from last year to do personalized learning using technology, or the district initiative to integrate literacy across the curriculum. And there's a state-wide initiative to increase college and career readiness. In your next observation, we'll be checking to see how you're doing with all of these initiatives!*

I wish I could say I was exaggerating, but many teachers tell me they experience "initiative fatigue." There seem to be so many competing priorities passed along from administrators that both everything and nothing feels important. In too many schools, trauma-informed practices and educational equity join the long list of initiatives. They are relegated to one-time professional development sessions or a brief mention in staff emails. When the next big thing comes along, old initiatives seem to be forgotten.

School leaders must be clear that equity-centered trauma-informed practices aren't just another initiative that will fade away. Instead, they're an essential value of how we do school. This isn't about creating a top-down mandate. Instead, leaders should make it clear that any mission or vision statement that includes the words *all students*—like "all students can learn" or "all students are valued"—isn't possible without a commitment to equity. Leaders need to live this commitment in everything we do.

Shared Values as Job Expectations

This commitment to equity-centered trauma-informed education can begin through a teacher's very first contact with the school. At Fall-Hamilton Elementary School in Nashville, Tennessee, principal Mathew Portell doesn't wait until teachers are hired to begin conversations on mindset. When prospective employees apply to work at Fall-Hamilton, the hiring committee sends them an information sheet about the school's trauma-informed approach, along with links to learn more. This information is then central during interviews, ensuring that a trauma-informed mindset is not simply "nice to have" but a requirement of the job, just as important as content knowledge or an understanding of teaching strategies. Similarly, hiring committees should specifically ask questions to gauge a candidate's understanding of and commitment to equity. At my school, we asked interviewees this question: "Students living in poverty are disproportionately identified for special education. How do you understand this?" Candidates' answers revealed a lot. If they focused on how poor parents didn't care about education or weren't interested in collaboration with school, we knew that candidate wasn't the right hire for our school. If interviewees focused instead on the systems that work against students in poverty and the structural barriers, it was a sign that they already had a foundation in equity literacy.

Once part of the teaching staff, teachers should be continually coached in implementing equity-centered trauma-informed practices, like the coaching I gave Tony during supervision. At the therapeutic school, unconditional positive regard was both a school value and a job expectation. We frequently talked about unconditional positive regard at whole-staff faculty meetings, but peer-to-peer interactions helped hold us all accountable. Mentor teachers who had been at the school longer helped coach newer teachers and modeled peer consultation that focused on problem solving and processing rather than complaining or venting. If our discussions about students veered too much into venting, we'd remind one another about our unconditional positive regard: "Hey, I know today was really frustrating. But remember, Corey isn't trying to push your buttons. You know he's working on expressing himself in a more thoughtful way. What can I do to help you plan for your class tomorrow?"

These gentle redirects helped create an environment where unconditional care for our students wasn't just something we talked about in one professional development session but was part of our everyday work as educators. When I became a leader in the school, this clarity of values-driven leadership helped me give feedback to my teachers. If one of my teachers was clearly stuck in a deficit narrative about a student or their family, I treated it not as just a difference of opinion but as an area for professional growth.

When equity-centered trauma-informed practice is a job expectation, we take it seriously if teachers refuse to participate in that growth process. Everyone learns at different paces, but as leaders we cannot gamble with our students' safety if we recognize that teachers are doing harm. There is sometimes a misconception that being trauma-informed means being touchy-feely or overly lenient. This isn't the case, particularly because keeping a safe environment sometimes means setting firm limits.

If there are teachers in our schools that are being harmful to students, trauma-informed and equity-centered leaders play an essential role through what we choose to do about it. I remember visiting one school in which teachers told me they didn't trust their principal's commitment to equity. When I asked why not, they told me about a coworker who regularly berated students, including making derogatory comments about their appearance. Yet this teacher seemingly experienced no consequences and continued to work in the school. If we are committed to equity, our intentional hiring practices would keep someone like this out of our schools. If we say we value equity and want to be trauma-informed, we simply cannot employ people who cause trauma. These are difficult conversations but ones that we must start to have if we want to change the culture in our schools.

In a parallel way to our work with students, holding high expectations for teachers requires that leaders also provide high levels of support. Two key elements of this support are mission-focused professional development and modeling your own learning.

Keeping It Focused in Professional Development

One way for leaders to fight initiative fatigue is to make sure that professional learning stays connected to your overall mission of an equity-centered trauma-informed school. Involve teachers in selecting professional development opportunities for the whole school, as well as curating content-specific resources and learning opportunities. At my school I created a structure for a teacher-led working group to plan each in-service day. We included representatives from different content areas and roles across the school. We then gathered feedback from the leadership team and from teachers about what opportunities they felt were needed based on our school's ongoing goals and initiatives. We would also consider the time of year, student needs that seemed pressing, and required certifications or trainings that were due, like first aid. Taking together all of these considerations, the staff group would draft a schedule and then invite feedback before finalizing it. The end result was an intentional schedule that included mandatory and optional professional development, down time, social time, and opportunities for staff wellness activities.

Involving staff in designing professional development or selecting outside trainers or organizations can also help keep professional learning focused. You might create a series of questions based on your school's stated goals or mission statement to evaluate any professional development options. If you are committed to developing your staff's equity literacy, any professional development facilitator you hire should also be committed to equity. For example, if you are looking for someone to work with your math teachers on integrating hands-on learning and manipulatives, ask the math consultant about equity considerations in their approach.

Recall the four proactive priorities for trauma-informed practice: predictability, flexibility, connection, and empowerment. This professional development model addressed them all: a clear process with predictable opportunities for input, flexibility based on the needs of teachers and the school, staff agency and empowerment to lead their own learning, and all of this based in our caring community. Trauma-informed teachers should have opportunities to experience trauma-informed learning environments. Focusing professional development around equity-centered trauma-informed content is important, and it's even more impactful when it's planned and facilitated in equity-centered trauma-informed ways.

Model Your Own Learning

If you want to hold a high bar for teachers in their work on equity and justice, you must model that commitment too. School leaders need to be lead learners of equity literacy and trauma-informed practice.

Like teachers, school leaders are responsible for examining their identities and how these identities impact their work. This is especially relevant given the demographics of school leaders. While over 75% of teachers are women, only 54% of principals and 23% of superintendents are women. Less than a quarter of principals and only about 6% of superintendents are people of color (NEA Research, 2019). All of this means that the makeup of school leadership is more likely to be male and white than the makeup of either the teachers or students in their schools. Leaders need to do their own work to understand what this means and how it affects their leadership. If we do not do this self-work publicly, how can the teachers we lead trust that we are really committed to equity?

Doing the work publicly might look like sharing out the books or resources that you are reading and what learning you take from them. When staff see you critically thinking about your learning and putting it into action, you model for them that they can do the same. This can be as simple as sharing an "aha" moment from your professional learning in a staff meeting or updating your team on policy revisions you are working on. There's also great power in publicly apologizing or engaging in restorative conversations with staff, students, or community members if you recognize ways you have harmed them.

In the context of the supervision meetings I described in the previous chapter, school leaders need to be aware of how their identities impact their supervisor-supervisee relationships. I remember one frustrating experience in which a student, in a moment of anger, had made a series of cruel anti-Semitic comments to me. I felt a whole range of emotions, including fear, sadness, and frustration. Memories of other times I had been targeted with anti-Semitism all rushed to the surface. A couple of days later I sat down with one of the administrators at my school, a white Christian man, to process the incident and seek support for how I would go forward in working with the student. In our conversation the administrator ignored how my identity as a Jewish person was relevant to the incident and instead focused on tips around vicarious trauma in general. I felt erased instead of affirmed and supported.

Just as teachers need to see, affirm, and support our students' identities, so do administrators and leaders need to see, affirm, and support the identities of our employees. Remember Principle 2 of equity-centered trauma-informed education: *this work is asset based*, recognizing the inherent strengths and capacities of not just our students but teachers, too. When my administrator minimized the importance of my identity, I felt like he couldn't see *me* and therefore didn't understand my strengths or my capacity for resilience. At that moment I needed my administrator to help me unpack the situation and process my emotions so I could move forward with a restorative process with my student. Because he brushed over my identity, I instead continued to feel unsettled and unsupported, which negatively affected my work with my student.

As school leaders we need to start with our own learning and reflection about how our identity shapes our work, and be transparent about what we discover. If you encounter a moment where you recognize you don't have the skills or background knowledge to support a staff member, be honest and help that person find other ways to get guidance. Being aware of how identity shapes our work is also a key understanding as we foster the leadership in our staff. For leaders to hold everyone to high standards around equity, we need to be sure we're not shutting down difficult conversations.

Value Feedback and Teacher Leadership

As a learning-focused, values-driven leader, you also have to make sure that you protect the teachers who are brave enough to speak truth to power. While many white teachers and school leaders have become interested in and invested in equity in recent years, teachers of color have been leading this work for a long time. Yet often when teachers of color speak out about injustice in their schools or take on leadership in antiracist teaching, they are punished.

In their article for *Learning for Justice* (formerly *Teaching Tolerance*) magazine titled "What White Colleagues Need to Understand" (2020), authors Clarice Brazas and Charlie Mcgeehan spoke with educator Marian Dingle about this type of backlash:

> *Sometimes, we heard, when educators of color do take responsibility for antiracist work, they pay a price. Marian Dingle told us that when she decided to teach in a more proactively antiracist way, she noticed a shift with her school's administrators. She had a stellar record, and she was being considered for a new position mentoring new educators. But suddenly, things changed. Her administrator accused her of not being a team player and questioned her competence. "The real issue, which was uncovered through layers and layers of questioning," Dingle says, "was that my administrator was uncomfortable with the way I was teaching." (n.p.)*

Just as teachers should be accountable for the ways we cause trauma for our students, school leaders should be accountable for creating traumatic environments for staff. As leaders we must value feedback and welcome the leadership of teachers who push for equity and justice, even—especially—when that makes us uncomfortable. The discomfort that white or otherwise privileged school leaders may feel when teachers speak and act against injustice is a cue for self-reflection, not retaliation. Why do you feel uncomfortable? What is it you're trying to protect? As leaders we should protect the teachers and students for whom we are responsible, not an oppressive status quo.

As leaders, we should make it a goal to foster leadership opportunities for our teachers who may frequently be denied or pushed out of them. If you notice that marginalized teachers are experiencing pushback for their social justice teaching, make it clear that you support their work. Lift up social-justice-focused and antiracist teaching practices as examples of work aligned with your school mission. Check in frequently with all of your teachers about what they need to feel supported. If teachers are criticized by parents or community members for justice-focused teaching, stand with your teachers and help educate the community about the importance of these teaching practices. Leaders must live our values through our advocacy for our teachers.

ACTION STEPS: LEADING PEERS AND LEADING UP

- *Speak up.* As a teacher, you know that your students need timely and rich feedback to improve. So do your administrators! If professional development feels unconnected to core values, or if you aren't receiving the support you need, tell your leaders.
- *Facilitate an affinity group.* Affinity groups are safe spaces for people with a shared identity to discuss concerns and experiences. At my school, we held a women's affinity group to process sexist comments from students. The affinity group helped us build a shared understanding of the problem so we could advocate for change. Affinity groups can also be a powerful experience for students and help them strategize for social justice action (Bell, 2015).

11 | Work Toward Policy Change

So far the chapters in Part IV have discussed how leaders can create school-wide conditions for teacher wellness and support the sustainability of trauma-informed work. One of the other essential roles of a school leader in advancing equity is to root out the status quo in its favorite hideout: school policy.

In the scenario at the beginning of Part IV, special educator Jasmine felt frustrated by school-wide policy when it upended the work she was doing to create a safe environment for her student Marta. As an individual teacher, Jasmine could not shift the zero-tolerance substance use policy. To best support Marta and all of her other students, Jasmine needs to know that school administrators are equally committed to equity-centered trauma-informed practices. One of the most important roles of school leaders is to use their influence in a way that classroom teachers are often not able to do and work for policy change within schools and districts.

The goals of school-wide policies should be to create conditions for community, learning, and safety. Embedding equity into policies ensures that equitable conditions aren't just left up to whoever happens to work at the school this year. Embedding an understanding of trauma into policies ensures that a school has the conditions to support trauma-informed practice of individual teachers.

Examining Current Policies

How did your school policies come to be? Who wrote them, and what were the values of those who wrote them? How long has it been since you examined your school and district policy through an equity lens, if ever? These are questions we need to ask about the policies and rules that govern our schools and, consequently, the lives of the students and teachers in our communities. Policy documents are statements of our values as educators. The policies that we put into writing are a clear articulation of how we want our schools to operate. If we hope our schools will be trauma-informed and equity-centered, our policies must align with that hope.

What kind of policies should we revisit? Any and all of them. Consider how students are admitted to AP courses. Consider bathroom access policies and cell phone use policies. All of these and many others can have a profound impact on creating trauma-informed, equitable environments, or on perpetuating inequity and traumatizing or retraumatizing students.

There is no perfect policy that will work in every single school, so I'm not providing you with sample policies here. Instead, Table 11.1 poses some questions to guide a reflective conversation on existing policy. Consider using these questions in a working group composed of students, teachers, administrators, parents and other family members and caregivers, and community members. Choose one area of policy, and use the reflection questions to uncover potential equity challenges with the policy.

Table 11.1: Policy Review Tool: Generating Questions to Critically Analyze Policy	
Use the reflection questions in the left-hand column to guide your analysis of school policy. The reflection questions should help you generate additional specific questions and concerns about each policy. These concerns can then be addressed by a group representing the different roles in your school community as you revise and rewrite policy.	
Reflection question	**Example**
What are the philosophical assumptions behind this policy?	**Policy:** "Minimum 10-day suspension for second offense of student substance use at school." **Questions:** What is the understanding of why a child or adolescent uses drugs? How does that understanding connect to a consequence of being out of school for two weeks?
Does this policy run the risk of being inequitably enforced based on the implicit or explicit bias of individual teachers or administrators?	**Policy:** "Students will be subject to consequences for insubordination." **Questions:** Could bias cause teachers to see behavior by Black students as insubordinate more often? Does punishing insubordination unfairly punish those who speak up against injustice?
What cultural values or norms are expressed in this policy? Are there assumptions of what is good, bad, appropriate, or inappropriate in this policy?	**Policy:** "Students will display courtesy and consideration at school events, on and off campus." **Questions to ask:** What does "courtesy and consideration" mean? Do we all agree on the definition? How will students know if they are being courteous and considerate?
As we currently enforce it, does this policy impact groups of students differently? Does this policy disproportionately affect students of color, students with IEPs, or English-language-learner students?	**Policy:** "The principal may call town police to assist if students are disrupting the learning environment." **Questions to ask:** Would a police intervention impact my students of color differently than my white students? Would a police intervention impact my disabled students differently than those without a disability?

Does this policy unfairly hold students accountable for factors outside of their control (e.g., access to money, resources, time outside of school)?	**Policy:** "After seven unexcused late arrivals to school, all future tardiness must be excused by a doctor's note." **Questions to ask:** What are the factors, outside of students' control that might cause them to be late to school? What are the factors that might make timely and reliable transportation a challenge for families? How should a family without health insurance proceed with obtaining doctor's notes?
How does this policy connect to our current understanding of trauma, safety, and mental health?	**Policy:** "Forging a parent's signature on a school document will result in a two-day suspension." **Questions to ask:** What are some possible explanations for why a child might forge a parent's signature? Might this alert us to a child's concern about safety, rather than being a sign of intentional mischief? If there is a possibility of a safety concern, how does suspension help or hurt?
What unspoken lessons does this policy teach students, staff, and caregivers?	**Policy:** "Perfect attendance will be recognized and rewarded by the school." **Questions to ask:** Does this policy disproportionately reward students who do not have chronic illnesses? Does it reward students with health insurance at higher rates? Are students who are absent because of a death in the family ineligible for the reward?

An overarching question to ask about any policy is, "Does this support a culture of care or a culture of compliance?" Policies do need to be clear, and there are often legal components to consider. But policies need not be harsh to be clear. When looking for policy examples for this chapter, I noticed that in one district handbook whenever the term *immediate family* was used, there was a note that said, "see glossary." In the glossary, the district defined who counted as immediate family, and restricted excused absences for illness or death to those predefined members of immediate family. How can a school possibly define for all of its students who counts as family, essentially defining who students are allowed to grieve? When I read this, I saw a school district with no trust that its families can make their own decisions on who or what is important enough for their child to miss school. Without trust, there can be no real community.

As you reflect on policies using the guide in Table 11.1, you may feel frustrated that some inequitable policies are dictated by federal or state law or by school board decisions. Remember that we can start within our spheres of influence and then work to grow that sphere. What are the areas that your school has the agency to change now? And how might you advocate at higher levels to change inequitable district policy?

Once you identify a policy that needs change, use the proactive priorities of predictability, flexibility, connection, and empowerment to guide you:

- *Predictability:* Policy should be able to be fairly and predictably implemented. Remove language that is too vague or up for wildly different interpretations depending on the reader (e.g., *disrespectful* or *insubordination*).
- *Flexibility:* Remember that predictable doesn't mean rigid. Build in opportunities for curiosity and empathy in any policy. For example, instead of zero-tolerance behavior policies where certain infractions automatically lead to disciplinary actions, consider restorative approaches where conversation with the involved parties is a key part of the process.
- *Connection:* Do the consequences of school policies ostracize students or increase their connection to school? Using restorative practices can be helpful in reconsidering our response to student rule violations. In restorative practices, there is a focus on accountability to the community as opposed to accountability to the rules themselves. Ask whether the consequences or procedure following a policy violation helps students repair their relationships in community or whether they are simply punishments for breaking rules.

- *Empowerment:* Student agency should be at the core of policies, so that policies do not become a way to silence student voice. The enforcement of any policy needs to include opportunities for conversation with the impacted students and a clear process for students, teachers, and families to appeal administrator decisions.

Imagining New Policies

Just as important as adjusting what is already included in our student handbook is considering what we have omitted. Handbooks are not the only way for students to get information about a school, but what you choose to include in the handbook speaks to the values of your school. Beyond the handbook, what is included and easy to find on the school website? What's promoted on social media? If we share information about resources only with students that the school identifies as needing "tier 2" or "tier 3" interventions, we are making an assumption about students who appear to be okay. When we make information about community resources and support public, we can create better access to these supports and destigmatize getting help.

How do students know who they can turn to for resources? Do they know which types of situations their school may be able to help with? I teach at a community college, and for the first few years I worked there I was unaware of a fund available to students for minigrants to help with such things as broken laptops or car repairs. Since most faculty didn't know about this fund, neither did most students. Resources that are designed to help students can't help much if the students don't know the help is available. Do your students and teachers know about all of the support available at your school or in your community? Do they know how to access resources for mental health, for food access, for low-barrier health care?

While it's important for counselors to have a full list of community resources and know how to access them, visiting the counselor in the first place can be a barrier. Make sure that these resources are listed in the school handbook and on the website and promoted on social media throughout the year. Teachers can be given time during staff meetings or professional development days to learn about these resources, ask questions, and hear from representatives of community partners.

Here are some specific areas to consider including in your school's student/family handbook and website. This is not an exhaustive list; instead, these are suggestions for how you can use your handbook and website to promote Principle 5 of equity-centered trauma-informed education: *taking a universal approach, implemented proactively*:

- *The process for referrals to mental health support within or outside of school:* Do students and their families know how to directly access mental health support at your school, or does the process rely on teachers or counselors identifying students they perceive to be in need? The school can help destigmatize mental health challenges by offering information to everyone in the school community on how they can self-refer. Include information about who is available within the school (counselors, social workers, school psychologists) and what community partners or agencies are available in the community.
- *Teacher-student boundaries*: Articulate any guidelines about how teachers are expected to maintain boundaries with students. Are teachers allowed to hug students? To share their home or cell phone numbers? To drive students in their cars? Review any relevant state or federal laws and policies, such as your state's mandated reporting law, as you create student-friendly language to explain what students should expect from their teachers.
- *Basic needs and accessing support for them at school*: Does your school have resources for families who need food, clothes, or school supplies? Don't wait for families to ask to make these things available. Put this information in your handbook (and advertise it often on the school website and in social media) on how to access food, clothing, and other supplies at school or at nearby community resources. Also include information on free meals for children in your community, and send out this information frequently before school breaks.

Policies and information for these items, and how to promote them, can be considered in a working group, similar to the suggestion above for policy review, comprising students, teachers, administrators, parents and other family members and caregivers, and community members.

Of course, the existence of equitable policy doesn't guarantee equitable practice. Schools need both policy that ensures equitable systems and leaders who ensure that school practice is equitable. We also shouldn't wait for all of the policies to be updated on paper before we implement equitable practices.

Working in Our Spheres of Influence and Causing Good Trouble

Creating an ecosystem of equity-centered trauma-informed practices will require systems change and collaboration across disciplines. Schools will need to work together with medical professionals, lawmakers, and community leaders. This is not easy work, and a lot of the work of systems change is outside of a teacher's control. If my students are overwhelmed with anxiety because of high-stakes testing, it's in my realm of control to teach them coping skills to manage that anxiety. It's not in my immediate realm of control to change federal and state education funding and accountability laws to decrease the pressure of testing on students. So, if I'm a teacher and I'm required to implement high-stakes testing, I might focus on giving students tools to cope with the stress and anxiety of taking the test. There's nothing wrong with that, but it's not trauma-informed to simply teach coping skills while never addressing the fact that schools are inflicting such stress. A true trauma-informed transformation would be to end practices that cause undue hardship. Teachers are therefore left in a bind: when I can't control the big stuff, all that I feel I can do is the little stuff.

Yet not all systems are so out of reach for classroom teachers. Within our classrooms and our schools, teachers have great influence over conditions that either create equity or perpetuate inequity. We return again to the idea of humanizing or dehumanizing classrooms. Teachers make choices about how to empower or disempower students within their classrooms, to enforce or push back against discriminatory policies, and to teach with a social justice lens or maintain the status quo. Will I choose to limit student bathroom use because I have the power to do so, or allow for the less controllable policy of just letting students go when they choose to go? Will I teach self-regulation skills so students focus harder on rote tasks, or create engaging and hands-on learning opportunities? Will I do the hard work of creating community in my classroom, or boil relationships down to points and demerits? Will I advocate for a misbehaving student to be suspended, or ask my principal for support to keep the student in my class? I am responsible for making these choices. If I care about ending trauma and creating equity, I need to own that responsibility.

Sometimes making these choices requires a little "creative non-compliance" (Meier & Gasoi, 2017). If a school district requires a practice or curricular approach that I know will cause harm to my students, how can I resist this requirement? Earlier, I mentioned that some schools provide students with limited bathroom passes and expect teachers to penalize students who exceed these passes. This is an equity issue: in a human-centered school, students should be allowed to use the bathroom—that is, meet their basic human needs—without restriction. For students with chronic illnesses or students who menstruate, for example, the stress of managing bathroom use can negatively affect their ability to be successful in school. One teacher I know, in a school with a strict hallway pass policy, simply doesn't require students to use the passes in her class. She chooses to allow her students to use the bathroom whenever they need to, even though it means risking her own job by breaking the rules. Her noncompliance with the policy doesn't change the policy, but it decreases the harm to students at the current moment. This teacher is engaged in equity advocacy on multiple fronts from her position within the school, but she chose not to wait for the policy to change. Teacher and author Cornelius Minor wrote about saying no to harmful policies and curricula in his book *We Got This* (2019), connecting this refusal to our core values as teachers: "Every classroom decision is a statement of values. I value young people, their communities, their interests, and their goals. My *no* statements reflect this" (p. 66). If we value equity and putting an end to trauma, sometimes we need to be noncompliant with directives that diminish those values.

Now, creative noncompliance can be a risk depending on our position within a school and relative power. It also comes with the very real possibility of being disciplined or fired, and each of us has to weigh the relative costs and benefits of this risk. We each have to make the decision that will work for our own lives, and these decisions can be influenced by our privilege and access to resources. These may buffer us if we face consequences for our noncompliance. But consider this: if we willingly comply with policies that we know harm our students, we are no "threat to inequity" (Gorski, 2018). In the words of US Representative John Lewis, sometimes we need to cause some "good trouble" in our fight for equity.

ACTION STEPS: LEADING PEERS AND LEADING UP

- *Start where you are.* If you aren't able to get involved in school-wide policy change efforts, start in your classroom. Teachers create classroom rules and expectations, which are policies too. Use the policy review tool to consider your classroom-based rules and start making change on that level. (In Chapter 13 I discuss cocreating a classroom community with your students.)
- *Get organized.* You and your colleagues have collective power to make change, whether you're in a union or not. The Labor Notes website (https://www.labornotes.org/) has tools and resources for organizers, including guidance on organizing around current issues and examples of successful actions by teachers and other groups.

Part V

Shift 4: Change the World From Inside Your Classroom

Teachers don't need to be therapists to provide powerful interventions for students affected by trauma. Sometimes teaching itself is a life-changing intervention. For students affected by trauma, school isn't automatically a safe place, but it can provide points of connection that help sustain a child through challenging times. Teacher Heidi Allum wrote about her experience with this in her essay "Trauma-Informed Teaching from a Trauma Experienced Student" (2019):

> During the most difficult times, if an adult had sat me down to talk to me about what was going on at any length or depth, I would have collapsed in grief. If a teacher was being visibly "extra-loving" or concerned it would have scared me. For me, coming to school meant I could do something else with my mind. I read vivaciously. I loved writing. And what I loved most was when I received actual, well thought out feedback on what I was doing with my work. That fed my fire. If I could do it, I could get out of the cycle of poverty, and be something. (para. 20)

Academic success was Allum's life raft in the midst of a traumatic childhood. As discussed in Chapter 8, our role as teachers is not to become a therapist. Instead, we should embrace the fact that teachers are one part of a healthy relational eco-system for kids. Alongside parents, family members, neighbors, friends, and community members, teachers are an integral part of a child's web of support. Our content areas and dedication to student growth are the unique thread we add to this web.

One of the most important things a trauma-informed teacher can do is *teach*. In our position as teachers, we can support students who are already trauma affected by building on their strengths, skills, and interests. We can also help prevent future trauma through fostering skills and competencies for navigating a complex world and fighting against oppression.

In many texts on trauma-informed education, recommendations focus on how to support students struggling with trauma to feel safe enough to access their learning. For example, in the guide *Helping Traumatized Children Learn* (Cole et. al, 2005), an oft-cited publication from the Massachusetts Advocates for Children's Trauma and Learning Policy Initiative, the following recommendations are made in the area of academic instruction:

- Using "islands of competence" to build on student strengths
- Predictability in routines and teacher responses
- Ensuring physical and emotional safety in the classroom
- Consistency in expectations for all students
- Positive behavioral supports
- Multiple means of presenting information
- Support to process information
- Identifying and processing emotions
- Referral to appropriate evaluations such as speech and language or occupational therapy assessments (pp. 61–67)

I like this list, and the resource it comes from has some helpful tips. But what's missing? The actual subject-area *content* of our classes. How might *what* we teach, not just how we teach it, be part of our powerful equity-centered trauma-informed practices? Looking only at how to support students' access to existing curricula makes trauma-informed practice too narrow an approach. It also isn't equity-centered because many of school's existing curriculum and instructional approaches don't enhance equity, and sometimes cause harm (remember the discussion of curriculum violence in Chapter 2).

With this in mind, I offer the fourth shift toward equity-centered trauma-informed practice: from focusing only on how the world affects our classroom to *seeing how what happens in our classroom can change the world*. We can partner with our students as change makers for a more just society. This final shift is necessary to bring about Principle 6 of equity-centered trauma-informed education: *being social justice focused, to create a trauma-free world*.

Earlier in this book I discussed a teacher's sphere of influence, acknowledging that we cannot solve all of the world's problems. We aren't solely responsible for the inequitable conditions that have created the hardships our students and schools face, and we can't be expected to fix all of them. This is important to remember so that we don't feel the weight of the world on our shoulders and become frozen by the amount of work there is to do. There's another way to look at our sphere of influence: the possibility that *our realm of influence is actually quite vast*, because we influence our students. One teacher impacts the lives of hundreds or thousands of children just through day-to-day work over the years. Through our role as teachers, we can facilitate students gaining the knowledge, tools, and skills they need to change the world. What could be a greater realm of influence than that?

There's a Jewish teaching that each person carries two truths, one in each pocket: in one, "For my sake the world was created," and in the other, "I am but dust and ashes." We reach for these truths at different times depending on what we need to sustain our work. Sometimes we need our courage to be bolstered, and sometimes we need a reminder to stay humble. What do we need to hold in our two pockets as teachers? For me, the slip of paper in one pocket says, "My circle of influence is my classroom," and the other, "What I do in my classroom can change the world." Holding both of these truths in our pockets, let's look at how we can create a world-changing classroom for social justice.

12 | Examine the Curriculum, Disrupt Harmful Narratives

"Don't tell students you believe they can climb the mountain. Climb it next to them and then point back and say, 'Look, we climbed the mountain.'" The director at the therapeutic school often shared this message with the teachers when we talked about student motivation. It was sometimes disheartening to listen to how students talked about their own capacities and abilities: "I can't do it," "I'm not smart," "I never get anything right." Students with these beliefs about themselves seem impervious to the positivity or optimism of their teachers, and this makes sense when we understand the harmful impact of trauma on self-worth. Trauma expert Judith L. Herman explained that children who endure abuse develop a sense that they are responsible for the actions of abusive adults: "Simply by virtue of her existence on earth, she believes that she has driven the most powerful people in her world to do terrible things. Surely, then, her nature must be thoroughly evil" (1992/2015, p. 105). Children's attempts to make sense of trauma often lead them to place the blame entirely on themselves when, in reality, children are never to blame for the trauma they endure.

Once in school, too many students then experience confirmation that their own wants and needs do not matter because the wants and needs of adults and the curriculum are prioritized. Bettina Love describes the importance of mattering, reflecting on how falling behind in school made her feel: "My most important tools—my opinions, my ideas of right and wrong—were in a holding cell. I could not find a space where I mattered" (2019, p. 47). Helping students build up their self-confidence isn't as easy as telling them "you matter!" or "you are important!" Instead, we have to create opportunities for work that actually *does* matter. We have to find ways for students to assert their importance to the school and to the community. This is the message of my school director's advice: rather than simply telling students "you can do it," we should simply get moving. When you look down from the top of a mountain trail, it's not possible to say "I can't do it" because you already did.

In an equity-centered trauma-informed school, we use both our actions and our words to help students feel a personal sense of power. This chapter highlights a few ways to do this through the lens of critical pedagogy.

Critical Pedagogy Is Trauma-Informed Pedagogy

Becoming an educator for social justice doesn't mean that we simply add some "social justice lessons" while leaving the rest of our curriculum and pedagogy intact. Instead, "social justice is humanizing our classroom environments so that all students not only see themselves, but also really see others" (White, 2018, para 4). As we develop our equity-centered trauma-informed lens, we transform our classrooms so that social justice is a driving force, not an "extra." Individual lessons that address social issues need to take place in the overall context of a classroom where students engage in real conversations about identity, race, and equality.

There is an abundance of literature and resources on teaching practices that foster social consciousness and justice. These approaches are collectively known as *critical pedagogy*. Critical pedagogy isn't something new: it dates back to Paulo Freire's 1970 book *Pedagogy of the Oppressed*. Even though Freire wrote this text half a century ago, his words remind me that we have not yet fully enacted a critical pedagogy in our schools: "Knowledge emerges only through invention and re-invention, through the restless, impatient, continuing, hopeful inquiry human beings pursue in the world, with the world, and with each other" (1970/2000, p. 72). Are our classrooms designed to foster invention and reinvention? Do we facilitate restless and hopeful inquiry between our students and the world? Do we encourage the growth of our students' critical consciousness, as well as our own? I know many teachers who do, but all too often they do this in spite of the educational system around them.

Culturally relevant pedagogy, as theorized by Gloria Ladson-Billings (1995), builds on critical pedagogy with a specific focus on the teaching practices that contribute to the success of African American youth. Elements of culturally relevant pedagogy include fostering academic excellence, cultural competence, and critical consciousness. Other scholars have extended and "remixed" Ladson-Billings' work into approaches like culturally sustaining pedagogy (Paris, 2012) and culturally responsive teaching (Gay, 2000; Hammond, 2015). All of these approaches share a focus on academic achievement, understanding and using cultural strengths in our teaching, and the development of sociopolitical consciousness. Perhaps most important, these critical pedagogies share an explicit goal of education as a tool for liberation and justice. The idea behind critical pedagogy isn't to help students of color be successful by dominant white standards of achievement but to transform education altogether so that schools are spaces of liberation.

Critical pedagogy is trauma-informed and equity-centered by nature because of this focus on justice and students' development of consciousness and agency. Education professors Kathleen Hulgin, E. Frank Fitch, and M. Nickie Coomer wrote that critical pedagogy "places human struggle at the center of curriculum and builds knowledge of how power operates in the world, with opportunities to question, disrupt, and shift the status quo" (2020, p. 14). Teaching with human struggle at the center positions students as leaders and partners in learning. This is the core task of Principle 6 of equity-centered trauma-informed education: aiming to create a trauma-free world.

I do not attempt to re-create a how-to guide to critical pedagogy in these pages. Instead, I highlight some key considerations connected to trauma as we implement critical pedagogy: building critical consciousness, disrupting harmful narratives, and navigating the complex issues of oppression.

Building Critical Consciousness

Why do bad things happen to good people? Most adults recognize that the answer to this question is complicated, shaped by our beliefs and experiences and our cultural context. Yet far too many children who experience trauma come to the simple and incorrect conclusion that bad things happened to them because they are bad. Trauma-affected children can develop the belief that they are essentially bad or defective, that they do not deserve love or care (Perry & Szalavitz, 2017). Similarly, children whose identities have been marginalized can internalize the negative messages they hear about themselves and people like them. In trauma-informed education, our job as teachers is not to provide therapy to unpack the deep shame or self-blame that each student experiences—that type of healing is a personal journey. Instead, we can help all of our students understand that individual narratives don't tell the whole picture. We can help build critical consciousness.

Critical consciousness is the ability to understand and intervene in systems of injustice. When we teach about systems of power and oppression, we help students understand how structural factors impact us as individuals. This can be essential for students who blame themselves for their trauma. It's not enough to tell kids, "It wasn't your fault." Developing a critical consciousness is a way for students to understand the complex ways that oppression operates and their place in making change.

The self-blame that students feel can be exacerbated by everyday messages about meritocracy. *Meritocracy* is the idea that personal responsibility is more important than community and structural factors, and this idea is so common that many take it for granted that it must be factual. For example, a common narrative of meritocracy is that students who excel academically can rise above their circumstances and escape poverty. Yet this is simply untrue as a general rule. According to a 2019 Georgetown University report, students with high academic promise from poor families are less likely to have upward mobility—that is, move to a higher income level than their parents—than a child from a richer family who performs worse on academic measures. The report clarifies: "The gap doesn't exist because affluent children are smarter than poor children—it's because income and social status provide access to environments that allow children to develop to their full potential, all but ensuring their success" (Carnevale et al., 2019, p. 3). Education is not an equalizer: these findings and others demonstrate that children's future economic success is more strongly related to that of their parents than to their own educational attainment.

When we repeat the false narrative that anyone can succeed if they just pull themselves up by their bootstraps, kids blame themselves for a lack of success. Research confirms that adolescent students end up with lower self-esteem and higher engagement in risk behaviors when they believe in statements like "In general, American society is fair," or "Anyone who works hard can get ahead" (Godfrey et al., 2019). These belief systems can send a harmful message that if you don't succeed it's only because you didn't work hard enough. This self-blame is harmful for trauma-affected students to internalize.

When we teach kids that structural factors are as important as personal choices, we help them make sense of hardships and adversity in ways that don't damage their self-concept (Hulgin et al., 2020). In the writing seminar I teach at my local community college, students write interest-based research papers. Almost every semester, at least one student who self-identifies as in recovery from substance use chooses to write a paper on the factors that lead to opiate addiction. Through their research, they find that there are many influences outside personal choice that lead to high rates of addiction: overprescribing by individual doctors, negligence by pharmaceutical companies, lack of appropriate health care for mental health, and more. Students often share in their end-of-semester reflections that they found personal meaning in exploring the big picture of an issue that impacts them personally, and a few students have even been inspired to find ways to advocate for change based on their expanded understanding. This isn't to absolve students of all responsibility for individual choices; rather, understanding structural issues helps students make sense of how those choices are shaped and impacted by systems of power.

For younger children, building a structural lens can be as simple as guided inquiry into the realities of our society. Third-grade teacher Ilana Greenstein (2019) shared an activity in *Rethinking Schools* magazine in which she helped her students develop a structural lens around wealth inequality. Greenstein divided a section of the classroom rug into five equal spaces, representing five segments of society, from the richest to the poorest. She then guided her students through a discussion to predict how wealth is spread across these segments, using 9,000 dried macaroni pieces as a visual representation of wealth so students could engage in a hands-on way. Students were shocked when Greenstein spread out the macaroni pieces to reflect the actual distribution of wealth in the United States, with only nine pieces of macaroni in the poorest fifth (representing 0.01% of the country's wealth) and 7,900 in the section of the rug for the richest fifth. Greenstein then guided her students through a discussion to make sense of what they had learned and connect it to previous lessons about fairness, equality, and racism. If third-grade students can engage in critical thinking about such complex ideas, just think what you can do with older grades.

Whatever your grade level or content area, you can help students develop a structural lens through guided inquiry of social justice issues. Invite students to question realities in your school or classroom: What factors lead to high grades other than hard work? What are the demographic patterns among our teachers? How does our neighborhood's history impact the school today?

When building critical consciousness among our students, we also need to pay attention to the ways that our schools may be reinforcing oppressive narratives. This is part of our own critical consciousness building as teachers.

Disrupting Harmful Narratives

We may have learned from Spider-Man that "with great power comes great responsibility." Sometimes, we teachers don't recognize the great power our words can have on the growing consciousness of our students. Consider the following hypothetical scenario:

> *Mrs. West, a kindergarten teacher, is monitoring her students as they have some play time at the end of the school day. She intervenes when she sees Brandon start to pull on Miriam's braids. After scolding Brandon and sending him to play on the other side of the room, Mrs. West turns to Miriam, who is visibly upset. "Don't cry," Mrs. West tells her, "he was just flirting with you."*

Socialization is the process through which we learn about the world around us and develop our beliefs, norms, and values. As teachers, we are partly responsible for the socialization of our students, and we have a choice to make. We can perpetuate harmful messages, like Mrs. West did when she minimized Miriam's distress and told her that it's normal for boys to express affection through violence. Or we can choose to disrupt these narratives so that they do not continue.

It may seem like an exaggeration to some to say that Mrs. West's comments contribute to trauma, but small comments add up. In this case, normalizing boys' harassment of girls is part of what's known as rape culture, or the societal norms that lead to an acceptance of sexual harassment and rape. Of course, Mrs. West isn't telling Miriam that rape is acceptable. But she is teaching Miriam that violence and love go hand-in-hand and dismissing Miriam's emotional response in favor of her classmate's assumed motivations. This is probably a message that Mrs. West didn't intend to teach. The messages we learn in childhood can shape how we interact with the world for the rest of our lives.

As with microaggressions (see Chapter 6), small moments can have a huge impact in creating trauma. One necessary aspect of being trauma-informed is to consider how we may be perpetuating dominant narratives of white supremacy, homophobia, transphobia, misogyny, Islamophobia, anti-Semitism, and ableism. If you read that sentence and thought, "That is a long list," you're right. There can be a lot to unpack and to relearn, but we must do it if we are to rewrite these narratives.

As teachers, we can do some of this rewriting through our curriculum, not just our interactions. We can start by helping students understand the basics: Who am I? What are the different aspects of my identity? How are identity traits like gender, class, race, and religion defined? Teacher Shana V. White engages her middle-school students in conversations about these topics and then extends student learning through activities that help students recognize their own bias, understand how different identity groups are impacted by issues like bullying, and explore what it means to be an ally. Students in White's class complete a final project with an identity portrait expressing their visible and hidden identities, and White says that the unit helps students "understand who they are, how they are unique, and how they can understand and support people who are different from themselves" (2019, para. 14). Empowering students to define themselves is critical to positive identity development, which in turn supports students' well-being.

Historical narratives are in need of interruption, too. Some adults are surprised to learn that the history we learned in school was inaccurate and that the inaccuracies contributed to harmful dominant narratives. Consider Christopher Columbus: Many Americans were taught in elementary school that Columbus was a brave explorer who discovered America. For Indigenous people, Columbus represents one of many Europeans who murdered their ancestors, forced their expulsion from their homes, and contributed to a collective trauma, actions whose consequences still resonate today. To be trauma-informed means that we cannot minimize or ignore the trauma of history, because historical trauma still echoes in our lives and our students' lives.

While some argue that children can't understand the truth about Columbus until they are older, equity-centered teachers have shown that children are ready and willing to explore hard history. Maryland elementary school teacher Nate Madden chose to face this topic head-on with his fourth-grade students instead of repeating the false narrative he had learned in his own upbringing. "I will not dishonor Indigenous peoples by repeating the lies that are told about them," Madden said (Schilling, 2019). Madden used primary source documents, such as Columbus's personal logs, along with teaching resources from the Zinn Education Project, which supports teachers to help students develop a more accurate and nuanced understanding of American history.

To create emotional safety, Madden intentionally built classroom community from the first day of school and frequently discussed emotions, their impact on learning, and how students can support one another in a classroom community. "Building that culture of care is so important when engaging with hard history with my students," Madden told me. He also selected or modified materials so that details were age appropriate, and he provided many opportunities for students to check in about how they were feeling, take breaks, or opt out. It's essential to consider emotional safety in the classroom so that trauma-affected students are not triggered in ways that prevent their engagement with academics. (See the text box below for additional considerations around retraumatization.) Finally, and perhaps most important, Madden also taught about Indigenous stories of resistance and resilience. Students learned stories of Indigenous people's strengths before learning history about harm and conflict.

After engaging with the facts about Columbus, students responded with shock and sadness at learning the truth behind the popular narrative they had been taught up to that point. One of his students commented: "This hard history made me feel furious!!! A reason for this is that Columbus enslaved people and killed them! He has made me feel this fury!" Another said: "It also made me frustrated because nobody with power did anything about it." They also shared a deeper empathy for Native people, both those directly victimized in the history they had learned and also those today who must witness the myth of Columbus's "discovery" and the erasure of his harm. One student summarized their learning: "If you do not know the truth, you will repeat the lie. When you tell someone the lie, they will tell the lie, and eventually the truth will fade away."

As a teacher, Madden facilitated this lesson in such a way that students used critical thinking to draw their own conclusions, while also disrupting the popular hero narrative. Elementary school students aren't too young to understand the complexity of hard history. At the conclusion of the lesson, Madden's students created posters celebrating Indigenous People's Day to hang around their school, and some wrote to school leaders to advocate for officially recognizing the holiday instead of Columbus Day.

This lesson is an example of an equity-centered trauma-informed classroom on a few levels. First, Madden supported his students in developing their structural awareness. Students discussed issues of power and representation. They reflected on how their own education has shaped their view of the world. This learning helps students develop their own sense of agency, understand oppression, and become active participants in working for social justice. For trauma-affected students, this sense of personal agency can be transformative.

You don't have to be a history teacher to be concerned with narratives about history. Everything has a history, from the development of mathematical concepts to the types of instruments included in school bands. Examining these histories helps students develop critical thinking skills, which in turn helps them to see and disrupt harmful narratives themselves. Consider how you can engage students in critical thinking about social issues in your content area, whether that means learning about the history of eugenics in science class or discussing the ongoing pay gap in professional women's sports as part of your physical education program.

RETRAUMATIZATION: A FEW BASICS

Retraumatization is when trauma survivors are triggered by a cue in the environment and feel like the trauma is happening all over again. In schools, students can become traumatized by their treatment by adults, but also retraumatized through topics and activities in the curriculum. Although we can't ignore potentially challenging topics in our classrooms, we also shouldn't needlessly trigger student experiences of trauma.

Provide Choices

Don't require students to share deeply personal memories or experiences. Always offer alternative prompts if you have an assignment or writing exercise that asks students to share personal stories. Let students write about fictional or hypothetical situations, and offer these alternatives to the whole class, not just certain students. Even if you don't ask these questions in your content area, you may have seen activities recommended to teachers such as "I wish my teacher knew," in which students finish that sentence on slips of paper and anonymously submit to their teacher. We need to consider whether these activities may actually retraumatize. I encourage teachers to adhere to a guideline from literacy professor Elizabeth Dutro: "making intentional space for stories of trauma is always posed as invitation, *never* as requirement" (2019, p. 38).

Reflection Questions
- In your content area, what types of personal reflection or connection prompts do you use?
- Could any of these prompts be potential triggers for trauma-affected students?
- What are alternative prompts that would allow students to choose their level of vulnerability?

Avoid Prompts That May "Other" Some of Your Students
I observed a first-grade classroom circle on a December morning. The teacher asked the class to share what gifts they most wanted to receive for Christmas for the daily circle prompt. One student sadly shared that all she wanted was to be reunited with her family. The teacher later told me that she was aware that this child was in a foster placement.

Reflection Questions
- How might that student have experienced her peers' responses in the circle?
- What assumptions was the teacher making when she asked students to respond to this prompt?
- How might a student who is Jewish or Muslim have experienced the morning circle?

Help Students Think Critically About When,
How, and Why to Share Their Stories
Storytelling can be a powerful healing practice, but school isn't necessarily structured so that sharing one's story will be healing. When my students choose topics for their research papers, usually one or two

students want to write about an experience close to their hearts; for example, a student whose sibling died wanted to write about bullying, which contributed to his death. I always ask students what might be positive about writing something close to their own experience, and what might be challenging? Students identify that personal experiences might make writing more engaging but also may make hearing writing feedback more difficult, for example. Helping students think about this proactively can give them the perspective they need to make decisions for themselves about sharing their stories in school.

Reflection Questions

- Imagine a high school student uses an assignment in her creative writing class to tell a story about her experience coming out and identifying as lesbian. How might telling her story be a healing or retraumatizing experience?
- How much does the student get to control her story and who gets to read it?
- How might peers affirm or dismiss her story in activities like peer editing?
- What might it feel like to receive a grade on such a story? Does it make a difference if the grade is an A or a C? Why?

Any time you invite students to share personal experiences in school, remember the considerations about boundaries and role clarity from Chapter 8: don't be a trauma detective, and be transparent with students about how confidentiality works in school. When in doubt, consult with the mental health support staff in your school.

Trauma Informed Doesn't Mean Trauma Ignored

As we discuss engaging students in conversations about difficult topics, you may be thinking, "Wait, I thought this was a book about trauma-informed practices. Aren't we supposed to avoid triggering topics?" This is a common misconception about trauma-informed practices, and one that we need to clear up if we are to work for equity.

Professors Brian Gibbs and Kristin Papoi conducted a study of teachers who had participated in trauma-informed training and who were also responsible for teaching difficult topics, such as teaching about war to the children of soldiers. They found that teachers interpreted the message of trauma-informed teaching professional development to mean that engaging students in learning about difficult topics is not trauma sensitive because of the potential for strong emotions and distress. If we understand trauma-informed practice to mean that we avoid all difficult topics, we are actually perpetuating trauma: Gibbs and Papoi wrote that "history must be taught honestly, or the trauma from the past will continue to haunt students as they move into their future" (2020, p. 109). The intersection of critical pedagogy and trauma-informed practice helps us navigate these complex issues and access the potential healing power of engaging in dialogue about oppression.

Of course, oppression isn't only historical. Part of a trauma-informed critical pedagogy should address what happens in the world around us and help students make meaning of it. Sometimes we can plan ahead for projects and units that dive into relevant themes. For example, a unit on analyzing implicit messaging about gender in advertising will be relevant every single year and can always be updated with current media. A unit on environmental racism can encourage students to take on the role of scientists and investigate water quality and air pollution in their neighborhoods. You can plan ahead for these types of units and projects and connect them with your content-area standards.

Other times, we need to be flexible with our plans so we can be responsive to what's happening in our communities. In *Rac(e)ing to Class* (2015), H. Richard Milner described visiting a school community where an armed robbery had recently taken place, during which the store clerk was killed. Despite students' clear desire to talk about and make sense of the robbery, teachers avoided any discussion of the events, citing fears that doing so would glorify violence or anger parents. Teachers also felt unqualified to bring up such complex issues or that talking about student emotions would cross the line into therapy. As Milner noted in discussing this case scenario, student concerns and fears will not disappear if adults ignore them.

Teachers should not consider current events or community crises as unrelated to content areas. Instead, we can support students through making space for emotional processing, as well as drawing connections between the curriculum and the events of the world. It can be a delicate balance because we also don't want to bombard or overwhelm students. Our classes can also serve as a place of respite and a place of shared joy. In my own teaching practice, I am constantly reflecting and evaluating this balance. I often check in with my students and gather their feedback.

Teachers should also be mindful of sensationalized narratives of trauma. Educator shea martin wrote in the essay "Our Trauma Shall Be Viral No More" (2020) that viral videos of violence against Black people, Indigenous people, and people of color sensationalize harm in the name of creating empathy. Reflecting on this "cycle of voyeurism," martin called for "sharing not only our trauma but also our resistance and resilience." Teachers need to highlight the stories of resilience, healing, and action alongside discussions of trauma. By learning about community organizers, activists, and social change movements, students gain models for their own work for change.

When we encourage students to investigate the injustices they see in the world around them, rich opportunities for connections in every curricular area abound. The tools we teach in science, math, social studies, and language can all be used in the service of justice. Dedicating class time to these projects helps position teachers alongside our students as coconspirators against forces of harm and oppression.

If you feel you can't deviate from your school's scripted curriculum enough to do big units or projects, you can still find ways to foster student critical engagement within the curriculum. If you are required to teach from an outdated textbook that perpetuates whitewashed history, supplement it with a paired text—there are resources on hundreds of topics available from the organization *Learning for Justice* and the Zinn Education Project. Teach students how to ask and answer such questions as "whose perspective is represented in this?" and "whose voice is missing?" When I read informational texts with my students, I ask them what sources were used and what sources could the author have used, but chose not to. Help your students see not only what's on the page or in the video but also what's left out. You can also engage students as critical thinkers about the very notion of how curricula are built. Take a few moments each week to discuss what was in the curriculum that week, and why students think the curriculum authors included it. Often, trauma-affected children learn not to trust themselves and their ideas because adults try to silence their voices. Teaching students to cultivate their own curiosity and critical perspective can help them regain trust in their inner voice. These are real-world skills that will serve students throughout their lives.

It's ironic because I sometimes hear comments from teachers, usually griping about student misbehavior, that we should emulate the "real world" within our schools. What teachers usually mean by this is that we should enact harsh behavioral consequences or deny students flexibility because "in the real world" employers and the criminal justice system are unforgiving. These comments are problematic for many reasons, but I most take issue with the implication that students are somehow not living in a real world. If we see our students as full humans, we also see their worlds as real. We must make space for our students to make sense of their worlds in our classrooms. This is how we can move from discussions about what students need "in the real world" to how we work together to create a better world.

ACTION STEPS

There is a wealth of fantastic social justice teaching resources online if you know where to look. Here are some of my go-to resources and texts:

Develop Your Lens
- Make it part of your personal professional development goals to seek out and learn more about critical pedagogy. There are so many incredible texts and resources on critical pedagogies, with more being created every day. Here are just three recent examples:

- *Culturally Responsive Teaching and the Brain* (2015), by Zaretta Hammond
- *Culturally Sustaining Pedagogies* (2017), by Django Paris and H. Samy Alim
- *Teaching When the World Is on Fire* (2019), edited by Lisa Delpit

• Near the start of this chapter I quoted teacher Shana V. White. Her essay *Lessons in Social Justice* (2018) is a must-read, exploring how social justice cannot be distilled to a lesson plan.

Transform Your Classroom

• *Learning for Justice* is my go-to resource for social justice teaching. In addition to the print magazine, its website (https://www.learningforjustice.org/) is chock-full of lesson plans, activities, and professional development resources.

• What's your check-in routine? Whether it's "rose and thorn" (success and challenge), a restorative circle, or a morning meeting, plan for taking a moment each day when students can share what's on their minds.

• One of my favorite equity-centered teaching strategies is the question formulation technique, which is essentially a question-asking protocol that facilitates student-led inquiry. You can find more in the book *Make Just One Change* (2011) by Dan Rothstein and Luz Santana or at the Right Question Institute website (https://rightquestion.org).

Shift the Systems

• There are efforts in states across the country to adopt state-wide ethnic studies curricula and standards. States with ethnic studies standards are ensuring that a socially just and culturally responsive curriculum is provided to every student. Find out whether your state has adopted ethnic studies standards, and get involved with ethnic studies advocacy at the district or state level.

• Conduct a school-wide self-study to examine the messages students get about identity and oppression during their time at your school. Is the development of identity understanding limited to one particular teacher who has a passion for the topic, or does your school use a systemic approach just like when building literacy or numeracy skills across the years? Take an honest look at where students are getting messages about race, gender, sexuality, and religion, for example. If you find that it's accidental or that your school doesn't touch on these topics at all, understand that students are still learning about these topics, but that your school isn't involved in the conversation. Get involved.

13 | Get to Work: Activism and Action as Healing

There is much work to be done in our education system to end the harm that students experience throughout the school day, and this work is ongoing. Yet, another truth is present at the same time: schools can be healing spaces.

The idea that schools and teachers can "heal" can feel uncomfortable—after all, teachers aren't therapists. To be clear, a healing school environment doesn't mean that we directly engage students in processing their trauma. Healing from a specific traumatic event or circumstance is a personal journey. As educators, we can help connect students to resources, but as discussed in Chapter 8, we are never in charge of someone else's personal journey with trauma. Yet school environments can be therapeutic without being therapy. In the nonclinical sense, therapeutic means healing. Think of a time when you had a healing experience without ever actually talking about what was bothering you, staying up late laughing with friends, for example, or a long quiet walk through the woods, or cooking a meal from scratch. These moments can be healing not because they directly unpack our trauma but because they provide us with moments of connection, peace, and joy. Therapeutic moments can simply be times when we are allowed to feel what we feel, to be fully human without judgment or expectation. There is also great healing power in the act of helping others and working for social justice. Taking action can help trauma-affected people move from being receivers of help to givers of help, from feelings of powerlessness to feeling powerful.

A healing school isn't about processing personal trauma. Instead, a healing environment is one in which students are validated, affirmed, and cared for, one in which students feel a sense of agency and the ability to make positive changes in the world. This chapter addresses the healing power of student action and leadership. This is another way to achieve Principle 6 of equity-centered trauma-informed education—*social justice, to create a trauma-free world*—by changing the world from within our classrooms.

Healing Justice

When people experience trauma, it can feel as if the world becomes a little more broken. Playing a role in putting it back together can feel like healing. "Healing justice" is a concept developed by Shawn A. Ginwright, which captures the idea that responding to trauma isn't simply about ending harm but about creating transformation and hope. In Ginwright's vision, adults and youth can work together to build "collective hope," or "a shared vision of what could be, with a shared commitment and determination to make it a reality" (2016, p. 21). When I think about the most impactful moments of my teaching career, I remember those times when the combination of teacher plus student plus content felt like alchemy instead of addition. It should be our goal as teachers to create classroom spaces where we learn alongside our students in the pursuit of a better world.

Let's not be mistaken: creating spaces where students engage in complex explorations of power, identity, and action is not easy or straightforward. In naming the "difficult truths" of creating such spaces, professor and researcher Kristen P. Goessling wrote, "Some days you will not get to the power analysis, some days will simply be about showing up and co-creating space for listening and sharing" (2020, p. 21). Not every moment is going to be magic, and we shouldn't strive for movie-worthy visions of overcoming adversity and toppling injustice. Instead, we can do what teachers do best: get to work.

Creating meaningful, real-world learning opportunities is one way to get to work. In his book *It's Not About Grit* (2018), Steven Goodman described the work of the Educational Video Center in New York City in supporting students to investigate the real problems in their lives and communities and to make change. In one student-created documentary, a student named Millie chronicled the toxic living conditions in the public housing where she lived, including rats and mold, and examined the landlord neglect that caused them. Millie then documented her community organizing effort with neighbors to petition their landlord for livable conditions. Through the documentary process, Millie was empowered as an expert, an organizer, and a leader in her community. Consider the difference between a school that laments about children's "home lives" behind closed doors and a program like the Educational Video Center that stands in solidarity with students and gives them the tools to make change.

A project like this is also a real-world task that requires advanced academic skills, including professional communication, storytelling, and original research. Students not only participate in a high-quality educational experience but also have the opportunity to practice their agency, working for real change on issues that matter. Of course, not all students are given the opportunity for projects like these. We need equity-centered trauma-informed systems change so that teachers have the support, resources, and funding to offer these types of transformative experiences for students.

Even if you aren't able to go out into the community with your students, there are still endless opportunities for activism within your school. At a school that I'll call Northeast Middle School, a student leadership group took on the project of overhauling the school's outdated and discriminatory dress code. The student group partnered with their local university to help students engage as action-research partners about issues that matter to their lives. The student group started by looking at the school's current dress code and identified elements that were racist or sexist, such as language about low-cut tops that placed blame on girls for creating a "distracting learning environment." Students also noted that the dress code was enforced in racist ways, targeting Black students for wearing head wraps and hoods. The students presented their findings to staff members at their school, who then had a chance to give feedback and suggestions on a dress code rewrite. Students also worked with their teachers and university cofacilitators to connect current academic research to their findings and help guide their decision making about the new policy.

Despite almost universally positive feedback on the new, equitable policy from students, family members, and caregivers, the student group faced a strong backlash from some their school's teachers. Instead of viewing this as a failure, students took it as an additional action-research opportunity. With the help of their university co-teachers, the student group conducted a feedback survey and then coded the results to look for patterns. Through this activity, the students identified language that demonstrated white fragility, discriminatory beliefs, and comments that expressed a need to control students.

Throughout this process, the Northeast student group practiced academic skills that middle school students are not usually taught, including understanding peer-reviewed research, conducting rigorous data analysis, and creating polished, professional written communication for a wide audience. An important factor in the success of the students was that the teachers of the group—both the Northeast teachers and the university coteachers—took a clear stance alongside the students and helped them apply a structural lens to the backlash from the other school staff. This stance transformed the way the students viewed the response. Instead of blaming themselves or being disappointed that their new dress code was not being enforced, students understood the opposition through a social, political, and historical lens. They saw how teachers uphold power structures and placed themselves in a long lineage of change makers who push against those structures.

When supporting students to take action, remember that student activism is not a replacement for teacher activism. We shouldn't put students in charge of fixing inequities as a way of absolving our own responsibility. It can be empowering for students to speak up about an injustice, but it's better if they never had to be harmed by the injustice in the first place. For example, establishing a Genders and Sexualities Alliance club in the school, linking with the national GSA Network, can be a powerful step to help LGBTQ students build community organizing skills. But you shouldn't wait for your school's Genders and Sexualities Alliance club to identify the lack of gender-neutral restrooms as a problem before taking action. I spoke once with a non-binary student who ran for student council on a platform of converting staff bathrooms into gender-neutral ones for student and staff access. The student lost the election, and the bathrooms remained inaccessible to students. We can applaud and uplift this student for their brave platform, but we should also take responsibility for the fact that the student had to advocate in the first place. The student should not have had to win their election for this change to happen. This isn't about a savior mentality that we must rescue our students or that they are incapable of self-advocacy. Instead, it's balancing that self-advocacy with the fact that the adults in school are responsible for creating equitable conditions. When you recognize that there is inequity or a trauma-inducing condition, policy, or environment in your school, you don't need to wait for it to cause harm before addressing it.

Helping Students Know They Matter

Change making doesn't have to be multiyear or multidisciplinary like the Northeast youth action project. Even in a single class period, you can engage students in action. It can be as simple as teaching students how to find the contact information for their congressional delegation or using the tools of scientific inquiry to debate whether or not cities should ban plastic grocery bags. We can also use small "teachable moments" to foster students' sense of agency. For example, you might be chatting with a group of students in the morning when one of them expresses her frustration that the school day begins so early for the high school. This can be a teachable moment to say to the student, "You're absolutely right. Did you know that most research suggests that later start times are better? Have you ever thought about writing an email to the school board?" This doesn't have to become a project or a lesson to be meaningful. Validating the student's concern and encouraging her to take action simply communicates that you believe her ideas have power and that the status quo isn't the way it has to be. For students to believe that they matter, we have to let them know, often, that their ideas matter.

One of the simplest ways to show students they matter is in the cocreation of classroom community. Often teachers determine the tone of the classroom, and the rules and the consequences for breaking those rules. If I tell students "you matter" but then scold them by saying, "You can't wear a hat in *my* classroom," the latter message wins out. When we instead establish that this is *our* classroom, and that the teacher's perspective is only one of many, we communicate to students that their ideas, needs, and hopes are truly important.

Fifth-grade teacher Jess Lifshitz (2018) accomplishes this by helping students critically look at the very concept of rules. She facilitates an activity early in the school year for students to explore whether rules are always fair, and when it's the right thing to do to break a rule, asking such questions as, "Is it worth getting into trouble for not following a rule that you feel treats you unfairly? Why or why not?" Based on that conversation, she and her students collaboratively decide how they will approach rules in their classroom. This gets to the heart of a trauma-informed approach by giving students the tools they need not only to feel empowered in the moment but also to build prevention of future victimization by helping students critically think about power and authority.

When we work to empower students, we understand that they are not the leaders of tomorrow but that they are already leaders with voices that need to be heard. Ginwright wrote that "healing justice is the result of both personal and political agency" (2016, p. 53). To create equity-centered trauma-informed schools, our students are our most impactful partners.

At the Crosswalk

The crosswalk in front of the therapeutic school was legendary. Our school occupied two small buildings, one on either side of the road. While the street didn't have too much traffic, it was a long straightaway and cars would often cruise by going over the speed limit. Crossing the street in that spot wasn't safe without a crosswalk. But the crosswalk hadn't always been there.

Several years before I started working there, a student at the school complained to her teacher that it felt unsafe to cross the road between the two school buildings. The teacher responded: "I think we can do something about that." Together, the student and teacher looked up information on the town website to find out which department was in charge of creating crosswalks. The teacher helped the student draft and revise a letter, and they sent it off to the town office. A few weeks later, students arrived at school to see the freshly painted white lines of a new crosswalk.

The most amazing thing about this project is the role it took on in the narrative about our school. Teachers and students who weren't at the school when the crosswalk was painted would point it out often, saying, "A student at our school got that crosswalk put in." The crosswalk became a symbol for student activism at our school. "Look," we'd say, "that crosswalk is here because of a student like you. What change do you want to make?" I loved telling new students about the crosswalk. I could see them processing the information as we stepped on its painted lines, filing something away for later: *the people here think that students can make a difference.* The crosswalk was a visible signal of our values as a school.

A crosswalk on a side street in a small town in Vermont doesn't change the world or end injustice. The advocacy process didn't fix all of the student's challenges in life. But it did make a concrete change in our community, and the legacy of the project has ripple effects that still touch students today. For me, as a new staff member, the crosswalk symbolized possibility. In a trauma-informed school, the past and the present are important. The challenging experiences we go through shape who we are. By creating trauma-informed environments, we recognize and honor those realties. But trauma-informed practices are also future focused. I learned from the story of the crosswalk that our school was a place where we helped students make their mark on the world around them. This sense of possibility shaped who I am as a teacher, and I saw it shape so many of the students who passed through those doors—and over that crosswalk.

In equity-centered trauma-informed schools, we acknowledge and witness the harm, trauma, and pain of our world. We create classrooms where students and teachers can be fully human: affected by trauma but not defined by it, hurting but also learning, struggling but also growing and already whole. And we create sites of possibility. We tell our students, *We believe you can change the world. Let's work on it together.*

ACTION STEPS

The best action step for student activism is to start with your students. They already have ideas about making change in your community and your school—just ask them! These resources may help you get started with supporting students through action and activism projects:

Develop Your Lens
- Fostering student leadership sometimes requires that we let go of some of our own control. Putting students in positions of power, after all, means that teachers need to be willing to not be the only one "in charge." Take some time to reflect on this, and be honest with yourself about where you are willing to share power with students. Try writing a list of 10 decisions that you make in the classroom, for example, which content to cover today, what groups students should work in, or the physical setup of desks. For each item, reflect on what it would look like for students to be part of that decision making, either in collaboration with you or on their own. This exercise may give you a starting point for inviting students into creating classroom community as leaders.

Transform Your Classroom
- Your community likely already has youth-led activism efforts. Learn about youth-led organizations or efforts in your area, and consider how you might connect your curricular area with their work, host speakers from these groups, or encourage student involvement. Creating these connections can provide your students with activist role models and opportunities to get involved.

Shift the Systems
- Consider a Youth-led Participatory Action Research project at your school as a way to involve young people in creating change in their communities and build their activism skills. You can learn more at the YPAR Hub website (http://yparhub.berkeley.edu/).

Conclusion

As an educator, I like questions better than answers. Questions fill me with possibility and allow me to dream and imagine. I remember sitting in my tenth-grade creative writing class when I first read Rainer Maria Rilke's words in *Letters to a Young Poet*:

> *Be patient toward all that is unsolved in your heart and try to love the questions themselves, like locked rooms and like books that are now written in a very foreign tongue. Do not now seek the answers, which cannot be given you because you would not be able to live them. And the point is, to live everything. Live the questions now. Perhaps you will then gradually, without noticing it, live along some distant day into the answer. (1929/2012, p. 21)*

Reading these lines as a teenager spoke to something I felt but hadn't known how to articulate: that the complexity and contradictions in life don't necessarily need to be resolved or simplified into one easy answer. I hope that you've seen through this book how closely I still hold that belief. Trauma is a tangled thing that resonates in our souls and hearts and bodies. Ending trauma is an exercise in loving the question, not seeking the answers.

In the spirit of loving the questions themselves, I'm not ending this book with a declarative statement of how schools might look if we were to fully implement the six principles of equity-centered trauma-informed practice. Although I've experienced some moments when each of these principles infused my environment, I don't truly know what a fully realized equity-centered trauma-informed school would look like or feel like. Even if I did, I hope that you will do your own dreaming and imagining. There are no one-size-fits-all strategies, and there shouldn't be any one-size-fits-all models for schools. The needs of each community are different, and our dreams for education in our communities should reflect that. So instead, I offer these questions, with an invitation for you to do some dreaming too:

- How would it feel to be a student in an equity-centered trauma-informed school?
- How would it feel to work in an equity-centered trauma-informed school?
- How would it feel to lead an equity-centered trauma-informed school?
- What would be possible if we made it a priority to affirm each person's full humanity in our school?
- What would be possible if we prioritized justice, joy, and hope in our educational goals?
- What would school be like in a world without trauma?

As you go about the everyday work of supporting your students and working for school change, I hope you also allow yourself time to day-dream and foster your own love for the questions themselves.

Standing in Solidarity With Our Students

Even though there are no easy answers when it comes to address-ing trauma in schools, there are some clear stances we must choose to take. Throughout this book, I have urged you to stand alongside your students in our collective work for equity and justice. On the most basic level, we can stand with our students through our uncon-ditional positive regard and a refusal to see students as anything less than human. But standing alongside our students will also require dif-ficult and complicated acts of advocacy. This means organizing to get police out of our schools and to fund counselors and mental health support. It means ending token economy behaviorist systems like positive behavioral interventions and supports (PBIS). Fighting for equity often means endless uncomfortable conversations with colleagues as we interrogate the biased philosophies underpinning curriculum choices or school policy. I know that I have sometimes felt exhausted by being "that person" to yet again bring up an equity issue to the administrators in my school.

Some teachers may worry about what it means to take a stand. What will happen if we rock the boat? Could we put targets on our back? Could we lose our jobs? These are real risks. Going against popular narratives that obscure oppression means that we are likely to receive pushback from those who want to defend those narratives.

School boards, districts, and community members often tell teachers, directly or implicitly, to be "neutral" or to "teach both sides." This can leave us wondering if we should teach about structural racism or homophobia, for example, and for some the risk of losing our jobs feels like a risk we can't take. These fears are real, and the risk can be greater for educators of color who get targeted disproportionately for calling out injustice. Even so, I call on all teachers, school staff, and educational leaders to consider the level of risk we are prepared to shoulder, and then to take that risk on behalf of our students.

Judith L. Herman wrote in *Trauma and Recovery* (1992/2015) that "working with victimized people requires a committed moral stance. The therapist is called upon to bear witness to a crime. She must affirm a position of solidarity with the victim" (p. 135). Teachers are not therapists, but when our students are the victims of abuse, racism, or discrimination, we too are called upon to bear witness. When we give equal weight to oppressive and hateful perspectives, or when we remain silent, we abandon our students and leave them wondering if their trauma is valid. Our students need to hear us say, "I believe you." Our students need to hear us say, "I am with you and I will fight alongside you."

To align ourselves with our students, we don't have to be partisan. Indeed, marginalized and trauma-affected students are not a monolith, and they don't share a political affiliation or a common view on all issues. Instead, we stand in solidarity with our students by affirming those conditions that uplift our students and working against those that oppress them. This means that we denounce transphobia, homophobia, and religious discrimination. It means that we oppose police in our schools and the use of exclusionary discipline. It means we advocate for equitable access to health care and childcare. If you feel discomfort in reading these statements, it's essential to reflect on why. To be trauma informed is to be committed to the end of the conditions that cause trauma. When we make this commitment visible to our students, we become true partners in the work for justice. My friend and colleague Dulce-Marie Flecha wrote powerfully about the need for teachers to connect the injustices of the world to the work of our trauma-informed classrooms:

> *Teach like there are children—children with mental illnesses, children living with trauma, children who have been kidnapped from their families, children who live at the crossroads of racial, ethnic, gender, sexual, ability, and body marginalization—who depend on you to model the justice that they are both entitled to and systemically denied. These children are not theoretical concepts. They are not tweets or Time Magazine covers. They are our past, current, and future students. Everyone committed to discussing and fighting the trauma systemically inflicted on children should also be committed to discussing and implementing the trauma-informed classroom structures that offer these children a more equitable opportunity for learning. (2018, para. 14)*

Flecha captures the "both/and" that I hope you take away from this book: we need to work on the big issues of injustice while also doing the immediate work in our classrooms. Teachers can't be expected to single-handedly fix large and complex systems like racism, sexism, and poverty. But we educators have more power than we realize, both individually and collectively.

As a classroom teacher, I can't single handedly change unjust laws that disproportionately affect my marginalized students. But I can help students develop the critical thinking skills to examine how laws shape our society and empower them to be active participants in our democracy. As a teacher, I can't end sexism. But I can teach students to recognize sexism in the books they read, the memes they post, and the television they watch, and give them the necessary tools to learn how to speak up against it. We can provide role models for activism and social change to help our students see themselves as leaders.

Is the creation of a more caring, less traumatic world too high a goal? I don't believe it is. After all, isn't teaching an inherently hopeful job? We help kids grow. We facilitate their imagining of the future even while we know that many challenges lie ahead. We can do this dreaming not just about our students' future but about the future of our education system as a whole. As Jeffrey M. R. Duncan-Andrade wrote in describing the concept of critical hope, "Audacious hope stares down the painful path; and despite the overwhelming odds against us making it down that path to change, we make the journey again and again" (2009, p. 191). Hope isn't just wishing that things can be better but daring to work toward making things better, even in the face of an uncertain future.

Throughout my teaching career, I have seen the incredible strength and resilience of my students. This resilience may not look like a Hollywood "defied the odds" narrative, and it certainly doesn't happen in isolation. Instead, I've seen resilience in the capacity for youth to ask for help, to give help, to stick up for friends, to restore relationships with family. I've seen this resilience in my colleagues and co-teachers as we find new ways to teach old truths, as we learn when to let go of what kinds of students we were so we can show up for the kind of students we see in front of us, as we get creative and get to work. And I've seen resilience in our communities, when parents and caregivers and leaders rally for schools because they hold out hope about the communities our schools can be when we invest in them.

There is a teaching I return to often, from the Jewish scholarly text the Talmud: "It is not up to you to complete the work, but neither are you free to desist from it." None of us will single-handedly end the conditions that cause trauma, nor will we rescue any particular child from pain or heal our entire classroom. Knowing that we can't or won't do it all shouldn't stop us from beginning. Throughout this book I have offered you many ways to get started. Remember that there is no checklist, and even if one existed, it would stretch out into infinity. Know that, even so, you can get started. Whether you've been on an equity-centered trauma-informed journey for years, or whether reading this book represents your first step, I'm glad to be on the journey with you. Let's get started.

References

Allum, H. (2019, September 6). *Trauma-informed teaching from a trauma experienced student.* Medium. https://medium.com/identity-education -and-power/trauma-informed-teaching-from-a-trauma-experienced -student-7d06ddad551c

Alvarez, A. (2020, June 30). Seeing race in the research on youth trauma and education: A critical review. *Review of Educational Research.* https://doi.org/10.3102/0034654320938131

American Counseling Association. (2011). *Vicarious trauma.* Fact Sheet no. 9. https://www.counseling.org/docs/trauma-disaster/fact-sheet-9-- -vicarious-trauma.pdf?sfvrsn=f0f03a27_2

Anda, R. F., Porter, L. E., & Brown, D. W. (2020, March 25). Inside the adverse childhood experience score: Strengths, limitations, and misap- plications. *American Journal of Preventive Medicine.* https://doi.org/10 .1016/j.amepre.2020.01.009

Beachum, L. (2020, January 24). Student will be barred from graduation unless he cuts his dreadlocks, school says. *Washington Post.* https:// www.washingtonpost.com/education/2020/01/23/texas-dreadlocks -suspension/

Becker-Blease, K. A. (2017). As the world becomes trauma-informed, work to do. *Journal of Trauma and Dissociation, 18*(2), 131–138. https://doi .org/10.1080/15299732.2017.1253401

Bell, M. (2015, May 13). Making space. *Learning for Justice,* no. 50. https:// www.learningforjustice.org/magazine/summer-2015/making-space

Berchick, E. R., & Mykyta, L. (2019, September 10). *Uninsured rate for*

children up to 5.5 percent in 2018. US Census Bureau. https://www
.census.gov/library/stories/2019/09/uninsured-rate-for-children-in
-2018.html

Bombay, A., Matheson, K., & Anisman, H. (2014). The intergenerational
effects of Indian Residential Schools: Implications for the concept of
historical trauma. *Transcultural Psychiatry, 51*(3), 320–338. https://doi
.org/10.1177/1363461513503380

Bornstein, J. (2017, February 22). Can PBIS build justice rather than
merely restore order? In N. S. Okilwa, M. Khalifa, and F. M. Briscoe
(Eds.), *The school to prison pipeline: The role of culture and discipline in
school* (vol. 4; pp. 135–167). Emerald. https://doi.org/10.1108/S2051
-231720160000004008

Brave Heart, M. Y. H., Chase, J., Elkins, J., & Altschul, D. B. (2011). Historical trauma among Indigenous Peoples of the Americas: Concepts,
research, and clinical considerations. *Journal of Psychoactive Drugs,
43*(4), 282–290.

Brazas, C., & Mcgeehan, C. (2020, Spring). What White colleagues need to
understand. *Learning for Justice*, no. 64. https://www.learningforjustice
.org/magazine/spring-2020/what-white-colleagues-need-to-understand

Brown, B. (2018). *Dare to lead: Brave work, tough conversations, whole
hearts*. Random House.

Bryant-Davis, T. (2018). Microaggressions: Considering the framework
of psychological trauma. In G. C. Torino, D. P. Rivera, C. M. Cap-
odilupo, K. L. Nadal, and D. W. Sue (Eds.), *Microaggression theory:
Influence and implications* (pp. 86–101). Wiley.

Carnevale, A. P., Fasules, M. L., Quinn, M. C., & Campbell, K. P. (2019).
*Born to win, schooled to lose: Why equally talented students don't get equal
chances to be all they can be*. Georgetown University Center on Education and the Workforce.

CASEL (Coalition for Academic, Social, and Emotional Learning). (n.d.).
What is SEL? Retrieved February 1, 2020, from https://casel.org/what
-is-sel/

Child Welfare Information Gateway. (2019). *Mandatory reporters of child
abuse and neglect*. US Department of Health and Human Services,
Children's Bureau.

Cole, S. F., O'Brien, J.G., Geron Gadd, M., Ristuccia, J., Luray Wallace,

D., & Gregory, M. (2005). *Helping traumatized children learn: Supportive school environments for children traumatized by family violence*. Massachusetts Advocates for Children.

Communities for Just Schools Fund. (2020, May 12). *When SEL is used as another form of policing*. Medium. https://medium.com/@justschools/when-sel-is-used-as-another-form-of-policing-fa53cf85dce4

Costello, M. B., & Dillard, C. (2019). *Hate at school*. Southern Poverty Law Center. https://www.splcenter.org/sites/default/files/tt_2019_hate_at_school_report_final_0.pdf

Craig, S. E. (2016). *Trauma-sensitive schools: Learning communities transforming children's lives, K-5*. Teachers College Press.

Craig, S. E. (2017). *Trauma-sensitive schools for the adolescent years: Promoting resiliency and healing, grades 6–12*. Teachers College Press.

Chiu, A. (2019, September 24). *Florida officer fired for 'traumatic' arrests of two 6-year-old students at school*. Washington Post. https://www.washingtonpost.com/nation/2019/09/23/girl-tantrum-orlando-classroom-arrested-battery-school-investigation/

Crosby, S. D. (2015). An ecological perspective on emerging trauma-informed teaching practices. *Children and Schools, 37*(4), 223–230. https://doi.org/10.1093/cs/cdv027

Crosby, S. D., Howell, P., & Thomas, S. (2018). Social justice education through trauma-informed teaching. *Middle School Journal, 49*(4), 15–23. https://doi.org/10.1080/00940771.2018.1488470

Curran, F. C., Viano, S. L., & Fisher, B. W. (2019). Teacher victimization, turnover, and contextual factors promoting resilience. *Journal of School Violence, 18*(1), 21–38. https://doi.org/10.1080/15388220.2017.1368394

Delpit, L. (Ed.). (2019). *Teaching when the world is on fire*. New Press.

Duncan-Andrade, J. M. R. (2009). Note to educators: Hope required when growing roses in concrete. *Harvard Educational Review, 79*(2), 181–194.

Dutro, E. (2017). Let's start with heartbreak: The perilous potential of trauma in literacy. *Language Arts, 94*(5), 326.

Dutro, E. (2019). *The vulnerable heart of literacy: Centering trauma as powerful pedagogy*. Teachers College Press.

Education Trust, & Cratty, D. (2019). *Fact sheet: School counselors matter*.

Education Trust. https://www.schoolcounselor.org/asca/media/asca/Publications/ASCAEdTrustRHFactSheet.pdf

Education Week. (2018, June 6). Survey data: School officers: Who they are; what they do. https://www.edweek.org/ew/section/multimedia/survey-data-school-officers-who-they-are.html

Eklund, K., Rossen, E., Koriakin, T., Chafouleas, S. M., & Resnick, C. (2018). A systematic review of trauma screening measures for children and adolescents. *School Psychology Quarterly, 33*(1), 30–43. https://doi.org/10.1037/spq0000244

Elliott, D. E., Bjelajac, P., Fallot, R. D., Markoff, L. S., & Reed, B. G. (2005). Trauma-informed or trauma-denied: Principles and implementation of trauma-informed services for women. *Journal of Community Psychology, 33*(4), 461–477. https://doi.org/10.1002/jcop.20063

Epstein, R., Blake, J. J., & González, T. (2017). *Girlhood interrupted: The erasure of Black girls' childhood.* Georgetown Law Center on Poverty and Inequality. https://dataspace.princeton.edu/bitstream/88435/dsp01tx31qm28z/1/girlhood-interrupted.pdf

Felitti, V. J., Anda, R. F., Nordenberg, D., Williamson, D. F., Spitz, A. M., Edwards, V., Koss, M. P., & Marks, J. S. (1998). Relationship of childhood abuse and household dysfunction to many of the leading causes of death in adults: The Adverse Childhood Experiences (ACE) Study. *American Journal of Preventive Medicine, 14*(4), 245–258. https://doi.org/10.1016/S0749-3797(98)00017-8

Flecha, D.-M. (2018, June 22). *Put your outrage where your classroom is: A pep talk to teachers horrified by headlines.* Medium. https://medium.com/@dulcemarie.flecha/put-your-outrage-where-your-classroom-is-a-pep-talk-to-teachers-horrified-by-headlines-2b6c58a30a83

Freire, P. (2000). *Pedagogy of the oppressed* (30th anniv. ed.). Continuum. (Original work published 1970)

Gay, G. (2000). *Culturally responsive teaching: Theory, research, and practice.* Teachers College Press.

Germán, L. (2020, May 7). *What I remember.* Multicultural Classroom. https://www.multiculturalclassroomconsulting.com/2020/05/what-i-remember/

Gibbs, B., & Papoi, K. (2020). Threading the needle: On balancing trauma and critical teaching. *Bank Street Occasional Paper Series, 2020*(43).

https://educate.bankstreet.edu/occasional-paper-series/vol2020 /iss43/10/

Ginwright, S. A. (2016). *Hope and healing in urban education: How urban activists and teachers are reclaiming matters of the heart.* Routledge.

Godfrey, E. B., Santos, C. E., & Burson, E. (2019). For better or worse? System-justifying beliefs in sixth-grade predict trajectories of self-esteem and behavior across early adolescence. *Child Development, 90*(1), 180–195. https://doi.org/10.1111/cdev.12854

Goessling, K. P. (2020). Youth participatory action research, trauma, and the arts: Designing youthspaces for equity and healing. *International Journal of Qualitative Studies in Education, 33*(1), 12–31. https://doi .org/10.1080/09518398.2019.1678783

Goodman, S. (2018). *It's not about grit: Trauma, inequity, and the power of transformative teaching.* Teachers College Press.

Gorski, P. (2018). *Reaching and teaching students in poverty: Strategies for erasing the opportunity gap* (2nd ed.). Teachers College Press.

Gorski, P. (2019). Avoiding racial equity detours. *Educational Leadership, 76*(7), 56–61.

Greenstein, I. (2019). Macaroni social justice. *Rethinking Schools, 33*(4). https://www.rethinkingschools.org/articles/macaroni-social-justice

Guess, P., & Bowling, S. (2014). Students' perceptions of teachers: Implications for classroom practices for supporting students' success. *Preventing School Failure: Alternative Education for Children and Youth, 58*(4), 201–206. https://doi.org/10.1080/1045988X.2013.792764

Haines, S. (2019). *The politics of trauma: Somatics, healing, and social justice.* North Atlantic Books.

Haines-Saah, R. J., Hilario, C. T., Jenkins, E. K., Ng, C. K. Y., & Johnson, J. L. (2018). Understanding adolescent narratives about "bullying" through an intersectional lens: Implications for youth mental health interventions. *Youth and Society, 50*(5), 636–658. https://doi .org/10.1177/0044118X15621465

Hammond, Z. (2015). *Culturally responsive teaching and the brain: Promoting authentic engagement and rigor among culturally and linguistically diverse students.* Corwin.

Herman, J. L. (2015). *Trauma and recovery.* Basic Books. (Original work published 1992)

Howard, T. C. (2019). *All students must thrive: Transforming schools to combat toxic stressors and cultivate critical wellness.* International Center for Leadership in Education.

Hulgin, K., Fitch, E. F., & Coomer, M. N. (2020, March 17). Optimizing a critical juncture: Trauma, neoliberal education and children's agency. *Journal of Curriculum and Pedagogy.* https://doi.org/10.1080/15505170.2020.1729903

Jackson, D. B., Fahmy, C., Vaughn, M. G., & Testa, A. (2019). Police stops among at-risk youth: Repercussions for mental health. *Journal of Adolescent Health, 65*(5), 627–632. https://doi.org/10.1016/j.jadohealth.2019.05.027

Jennings, P. A. (2019). *The trauma-sensitive classroom: Building resilience with compassionate teaching.* Norton.

Jones, S. P. (2019, November 25). Ending curriculum violence. *Learning for Justice,* no. 64. https://www.learningforjustice.org/magazine/spring-2020/ending-curriculum-violence

Khasnabis, D., & Goldin, S. (2020). Don't be fooled, trauma is a systemic problem: Trauma as a case of weaponized educational innovation. *Bank Street College of Education, 2020*(43). https://www.bankstreet.edu/research-publications-policy/occasional-paper-series/ops-43/dont-be-fooled/

Knestrict, T. (2019). *Controlling our children: Hegemony and deconstructing the positive behavioral intervention support model.* Peter Lang.

Kohn, A. (2005). *Unconditional teaching.* Alfie Kohn. https://www.alfiekohn.org/article/unconditional-teaching/

Ladson-Billings, G. (1995). But that's just good teaching! The case for culturally relevant pedagogy. *Theory Into Practice, 34*(3), 159–165.

Lehmann, C. (2016, December 5). *The ethic of care is hard.* Practical Theory. http://practicaltheory.org/blog/2016/12/05/the-ethic-of-care-is-hard/

Lehmann, C., & Chase, Z. (2015). *Building school 2.0: How to create the schools we need.* Jossey-Bass.

Lever, N., Mathis, E., & Mayworm, A. (2017). School mental health is not just for students: Why teacher and school staff wellness matters. *Report on Emotional and Behavioral Disorders in Youth, 17*(1), 6–12.

Lifshitz, J. (2018, July 21). *On compliance: Shifting the narrative from day*

1. Crawling Out of the Classroom. https://crawlingoutoftheclassroom .wordpress.com/2018/07/21/on-compliance-shifting-the-narrative -from-day-1/

Lipsky, L. van D. (2009). *Trauma stewardship: An everyday guide to caring for self while caring for others.* With C. Burk. Berrett-Koehler.

López, F. A. (2017). Altering the trajectory of the self-fulfilling prophecy: Asset-based pedagogy and classroom dynamics. *Journal of Teacher Education, 68*(2), 193–212. https://doi.org/10.1177/0022487116685751

Love, B. (2019). *We want to do more than survive: Abolitionist teaching and the pursuit of educational freedom.* Beacon Press.

Madda, M. J. (2019, May 15). *Dena Simmons: Without context, social-emotional learning can backfire.* EdSurge. https://www.edsurge.com/ news/2019-05-15-dena-simmons-without-context-social-emotional -learning-can-backfire

Marsh, V. L. (2018). *Bullying in school: Prevalence, contributing factors, and interventions.* Center for Urban Education Success. https://www .rochester.edu/warner/cues/wp-content/uploads/2019/01/bullying_ FINAL.pdf

martin, shea. (2020, May 26). *Our trauma shall be viral no more: Reflecting on voyeurism as a gateway to allyship.* Medium. https://medium.com/@ sheathescholar/our-trauma-shall-be-viral-no-more-b46ae94bc208

Masten, A. S. (2018). Resilience theory and research on children and families: Past, present, and promise. *Journal of Family Theory and Review, 10*(1), 12–31. https://doi.org/10.1111/jftr.12255

McNeal, L. R. (2016). Managing our blind spot: The role of bias in the school-to-prison pipeline. *Arizona State Law Journal, 48*(2), 285–311.

Meier, D., & Gasoi, E. (2017). *These schools belong to you and me: Why we can't afford to abandon our public schools.* Beacon Press.

Milner, H. R. (2015). *Rac(e)ing to class: Confronting poverty and race in schools and classrooms.* Harvard Education Press.

Minor, C. (2019). *We got this: Equity, access, and the quest to be who our students need us to be.* Heinemann.

Moore, S. E., Norman, R. E., Suetani, S., Thomas, H. J., Sly, P. D., & Scott, J. G. (2017). Consequences of bullying victimization in childhood and adolescence: A systematic review and meta-analysis. *World Journal of Psychiatry, 7*(1), 60–76. https://doi.org/10.5498/wjp.v7.i1.60

Morris, M. W. (2018). *Pushout: The criminalization of Black girls in schools.* The New Press.

Nadal, K. L. (2018). *Microaggressions and traumatic stress: Theory, research, and clinical treatment.* American Psychological Association. https://doi .org/10.1037/0000073-000

National Center for Education Statistics. (2019). *Fast facts: Teacher characteristics and trends.* Institute of Education Sciences. https://nces.ed.gov/ fastfacts/display.asp?id=28

National Child Traumatic Stress Network. (2011). *Secondary traumatic stress: A fact sheet for child-serving professionals.* Secondary Traumatic Stress Committee. https://www.nctsn.org/resources/secondary -traumatic-stress-fact-sheet-child-serving-professionals

National Child Traumatic Stress Network. (2012). *The twelve core concepts: Concepts for understanding traumatic stress responses in children and families.* NCTSN Core Curriculum on Childhood Trauma Task Force.

National Equity Project. (n.d.). *Educational equity: A definition.* Retrieved December 9, 2019, from https://www.nationalequityproject.org/ education-equity-definition

NEA Research. (2019, June). *Data brief: Diversity and representation in PK-12 education administration.* National Education Association, Center for Enterprise Strategy. http://www.nea.org/assets/docs/NBI%20 111%20Administrator%20Diversity.pdf

Noddings, N. (2002). *Educating moral people: A caring alternative to character education.* Teachers College Press

Nowicki, J. (2019). Federal Data and Resources on Restraint and Seclusion, House of Representatives. Retrieved from https://www.gao.gov/ products/GAO-19-418T.

Ossa, F. C., Pietrowsky, R., Bering, R., & Kaess, M. (2019). Symptoms of posttraumatic stress disorder among targets of school bullying. *Child and Adolescent Psychiatry and Mental Health, 13*(1), no. 43. https://doi .org/10.1186/s13034-019-0304-1

Paris, D. (2012). Culturally sustaining pedagogy: A needed change in stance, terminology, and practice. *Educational Researcher, 41*(3), 93–97.

Paris, D., & Alim, H. S. (Eds.). (2017). *Culturally sustaining pedagogies:*

Teaching and learning for justice in a changing world. Teachers College Press.

Pember, M. A. (2019, March 8). Death by civilization. *The Atlantic.* https://www.theatlantic.com/education/archive/2019/03/traumatic -legacy-indian-boarding-schools/584293/

Perfect, M. M., Turley, M. R., Carlson, J. S., Yohanna, J., & Saint Gilles, M. P. (2016). School-related outcomes of traumatic event exposure and traumatic stress symptoms in students: A systematic review of research from 1990 to 2015. *School Mental Health, 8*(1), 7–43. https:// doi.org/10.1007/s12310-016-9175-2

Perry, B. D., & Szalavitz, M. (2017). *The boy who was raised as a dog, and other stories from a child psychiatrist's notebook: What traumatized children can teach us about loss, love, and healing.* Basic Books.

Reno, G. D., Friend, J., Caruthers, L., & Smith, D. (2017). Who's getting targeted for behavioral interventions? Exploring the connections between school culture, positive behavior support, and elementary student achievement. *Journal of Negro Education, 86*(4), 423–438. https://doi.org/10.7709/jnegroeducation.86.4.0423

Rilke, R. M. (2012). *Letters to a young poet.* Dover. (Original work published 1929)

Rogers, C. R. (1957). The necessary and sufficient conditions of therapeutic personality change. *Journal of Consulting Psychology, 21*(2), 95–103. https://doi.org/10.1037/h0045357

Romero, V. E., Robertson, R., & Warner, A. (2018). *Building resilience in students impacted by adverse childhood experiences: A whole-staff approach.* Corwin.

Sabataso, J. (2020, February 18). Feeling "everything and nothing": Understanding curriculum violence in schools. *Rutland Herald.* https:// www.rutlandherald.com/news/local/feeling-everything-and-nothing -understanding-curriculum-violence-in-schools/article_f0638c15-11fc -50f7-aa17-a92bc527f460.html

Sacks, V., & Murphey, D. (2018). *The prevalence of adverse childhood experiences, nationally, by state, and by race or ethnicity.* Child Trends. https:// www.childtrends.org/publications/prevalence-adverse-childhood -experiences-nationally-state-race-ethnicity

Saunders, B. E., & Adams, Z. W. (2014). Epidemiology of traumatic experiences in childhood. *Child and Adolescent Psychiatric Clinics of North America, 23*(2), 167–184. https://doi.org/10.1016/j.chc.2013.12.003

Sawchuk, S. (2019, October 2). What districts should know about policing school police. *Education Week.* https://www.edweek.org/ew/articles/2019/10/02/what-districts-should-know-about-policing-school.html?r=57451633&mkey=93B95AF6-110F-463C-84FA-32A12A586A6D

Schilling, V. (2019, October 24). *"I will not lie to my students." Teacher's real history of Columbus tweets go viral.* Indian Country Today. https://indiancountrytoday.com/news/i-will-not-lie-to-my-students-teacher-s-real-history-of-columbus-tweets-go-viral-O4Oz-pMIQk2-7liFGotIlg

Shalaby, C. (2017). *Troublemakers: Lessons in freedom from young children at school.* New Press.

Semuels, A. (2016, August 25). *Good school, rich school; bad school, poor school.* The Atlantic. https://www.theatlantic.com/business/archive/2016/08/property-taxes-and-unequal-schools/497333/

Simmons, D. (2020, May). The trauma we don't see. *Educational Leadership, 77*(8), 88–89.

Smith, C. P., & Freyd, J. J. (2014). Institutional betrayal. *American Psychologist, 69*(6), 575–587. https://doi.org/10.1037/a0037564

Souers, K., & Hall, P. A. (2016). *Fostering resilient learners: Strategies for creating a trauma-sensitive classroom.* ASCD.

Sporleder, J., & Forbes, H. T. (2016). *The trauma-informed school: A step-by-step implementation guide for administrators and school personnel.* Beyond Consequences Institute.

Stovall, D. (2018). Are we ready for "school" abolition? Thoughts and practices of radical imaginary in education. *Taboo: The Journal of Culture and Education, 17*(1). https://doi.org/10.31390/taboo.17.1.06

Stratford, B., Cook, E., Hanneke, R., Katz, E., Seok, D., Steed, H., Fulks, E., Lessans, A., & Temkin, D. (2020). A scoping review of school-based efforts to support students who have experienced trauma. *School Mental Health.* https://doi.org/10.1007/s12310-020-09368-9

Substance Abuse and Mental Health Services Administration. (2014, October). *SAMHSA's concept of trauma and guidance for a trauma-informed*

approach (HHS Publication No. SMA14-4884). https://store.samhsa
.gov/product/SAMHSA-s-Concept-of-Trauma-and-Guidance-for-a
-Trauma-Informed-Approach/SMA14-4884

Thomas, M. S., Crosby, S., & Vanderhaar, J. (2019). Trauma-informed
practices in schools across two decades: An interdisciplinary review of
research. *Review of Research in Education, 43*(1), 422–452. https://doi
.org/10.3102/0091732X18821123

Thomas-Skaf, B. A., & Jenney, A. (2020, May 22). Bringing social justice into focus: "Trauma-informed" work with children with disabilities. *Child Care in Practice.* https://doi.org/10.1080/13575279.2020
.1765146

Torres, C. (2019). Mindfulness won't save us. Fixing the system will.
ASCD Education Update, 61(5). http://www.ascd.org/publications/
newsletters/education-update/may19/vol61/num05/Mindfulness
-Won't-Save-Us.-Fixing-the-System-Will..aspx

Van der Kolk, B. A. (2015). *The body keeps the score: Brain, mind and body
in the healing of trauma.* Penguin Books.

Varghese, R., Quiros, L., & Berger, R. (2018). Reflective practices for
engaging in trauma-informed culturally competent supervision. *Smith
College Studies in Social Work, 88*(2), 135–151. https://doi.org/10
.1080/00377317.2018.1439826

Venet, A. S. (2019a, August 16). *I have some questions.* Unconditional
Learning. https://unconditionallearning.org/2019/08/16/2224/.

Venet, A. S. (2019b). Role-clarity and boundaries for trauma-informed
teachers. *Educational Considerations, 44*(2). https://doi.org/10
.4148/0146-9282.2175

Wang, S., Rubie-Davies, C. M., & Meissel, K. (2018). A systematic review
of the teacher expectation literature over the past 30 years. *Educational Research and Evaluation, 24*(3–5), 124–179. https://doi.org/10
.1080/13803611.2018.1548798

Watson, J. C. (2017). Examining the relationship between self-esteem,
mattering, school connectedness, and wellness among middle school
students. *Professional School Counseling, 21*(1), 108-118 https://doi
.org/10.5330/1096-2409-21.1.108

Wheatley, M. J. (2006). *Leadership and the new science: Discovering order
in a chaotic world* (3rd ed.). Berrett-Koehler.

Whitaker, A., Torres-Guillen, S., Morton, M., Jordan, H., Coyle, S., Mann, A., & Sun, W.-L. (2019). *Cops and no counselors: How the lack of school mental health staff is harming students.* Retrieved from American Civil Liberties Union website: https://www. aclu . . . .

White, S. V. (2018, December 2). *Lessons in social justice . . .* Medium. https://medium.com/identity-education-and-power/lessons-in-social -justice-9add44ece4ed

White, S. V. (2019, October 9). *Creating a learning environment where all kids feel valued.* Edutopia. https://www.edutopia.org/article/creating -learning-environment-where-all-kids-feel-valued

Whitney, D. G., & Peterson, M. D. (2019). US national and state-level prevalence of mental health disorders and disparities of mental health care use in children. *JAMA Pediatrics, 173*(4), 389–391. https://doi .org/10.1001/jamapediatrics.2018.5399

Winninghoff, A. (2020). *Trauma by numbers: Warnings against the use of ACE scores in trauma-informed schools.* Bank Street Occasional Paper Series, no. 43. https://educate.bankstreet.edu/occasional-paper-series/ vol2020/iss43/4/

Yoon, I. H. (2019). Haunted trauma narratives of inclusion, race, and disability in a school community. *Educational Studies, 55*(4), 420–435. https://doi.org/10.1080/00131946.2019.1629926

YouthTruth. (2018). *Learning from student voice: Bullying today.* https:// youthtruthsurvey.org/bullying-today/

Index

Center on Poverty and Inequality
at Georgetown Law, 91–92
Centers for Disease Control and
Prevention
in ACE Study, 47
change(s)
from inside classrooms, 157–87
Chase, Z., 119–20
childhood trauma. *see also under*
trauma
case example, 157–58
in children with disabilities, xvi
impact of, 7
measurement of, xvi
as more than a number, 47–53
ongoing stress as, xvi
prevalence of, xvi
race and, xvi
relevance of, xi–xvii
resilience after, xvi–xvii
resources on, xx
children. *see also* Indigenous
children; *specific types, e.g.,*
disabled children
fostering emotional well-being
and resilience of, 70–71
mental health disorders in, 62
trauma in (*see* childhood trauma)
Child Trauma Academy, 7
classroom(s)
changes from inside, 157–87
trauma-informed, 83–95
unconditional positive regard in,
97–107
"clear is kind," 89
client-centered psychotherapy,

97–98
Coalition for Academic, Social,
and Emotional Learning
(CASEL)
competencies for SEL focus of,
60–62
Columbus, C.
historical narratives about, 168–70
community(ies)
equity-centered trauma-informed practices focus on, 63
in healing from trauma, xvii
marginalized, 8
students connecting with,
116–17
in wellness, 58–59
community connections, 116–17
connection(s), 109–21
action steps, 80t, 120–21
being proactive about, 71,
115–18
community-based opportunities
for, 116–17
don't be "only one" in making,
113–15
don't be trauma detective in
making, 110–13
gaps related to, 119–20
making, 109–21
in school-wide policies, 151
types of, 115–18
in universal approach to decision
making, 70–72
connection builders
trauma-informed teachers as,
115–18

savior mentality (*continued*)
from deficit views to, 88–90
described, 82
operating from, 113
in relationship building, 86–96
road to, 88–90
shift away from, 89–90
unconditional mentality *vs.*, 98,
98*t*–99*t*
to unconditional positive regard,
82
schizophrenia
paranoid, xv–xvi
school(s)
"bringing trauma to," 27
bullying in, 28–29
changes needed in, 15–17
contributing to social conditions
causing trauma, 8, 9, 27–34
counseling support in, 11–12
equity-centered trauma-informed, 142–43
equity-centered trauma-informed education for adults
in, xxi
harassment in, 28–29
harm caused by, 27–34
as healing spaces, 179–87
humanizing of, 58
Indigenous children's trauma-in-
duced events related to, 57
inequity in (*see* inequity in schools)
marijuana use in, 123–24
police violence in, 30
policy changes in, 147–56 (*see
also* school-wide policies)

racism in, 91–93
responses to sexual assault, 9
responses to sexual violence, 9
safety in, 57–58
SROs in, 29–32
trauma caused by, 27–34
trauma presence in, 55–58
trauma-sensitive, 4
trust in, 57–58
School-Based Health Alliance, 66
school-based racial trauma
types of, 33
school funding
inequitable allocation of
resources in, 11
school handbook
for school-wide policies,
153–54 (*see also* school-wide
policies)
school leaders. *see also* educator(s);
teacher(s)
accountability for creating traumatic environments for staff,
145–46
awareness of impact on supervisor-supervisee relationships,
144
teacher wellness responsibilities
of, 127–38
School Reform Initiative, 137
school resource officers (SROs),
29–32
contributing to school-to-prison
pipeline, 31
school system(s)
as perpetrators of trauma, 10

trauma (*continued*)
dehumanization and, 58
described, xvii, 6
discrimination-related, 8, 22–23
events/conditions causing, 6–9,
68
healing from, xvii
high achievement masking, xv–
xvi, 65
historical, 7
how we experience, 50–51
impacts of, 34–36, 40, 74–75
inequity in schools causing and
worsening, 27–34
lack of equity causing, 26
as lens, not label, 43–44, 55–66
making connections related to,
109–21 (*see also under* connec-
tion(s))
marginalized communities experience of, 8
as more than a number, 47–54
(*see also under* trauma-informed education)
as ongoing environment, 7
powerlessness resulting from, 68
presence in schools, 55–58
priorities related to, 67–80 (*see
also* proactive priorities for
decision making)
PTSD *vs.,* 6
"pushing past it," xvi
racial (*see* racial trauma; racism)
recovering from, xvii
relationships in recovery from,
83–95

relevance of, xvi–xvii
resilience against impacts of, 40,
74–75
respecting boundaries related to,
109–21 (*see also under* bound-
ary(ies))
schools contributing to social
conditions causing, 8, 9,
27–34
schools systems and educators as
perpetrators of, 10
sensationalized narratives of, 174
as structural issue, 8–9
teachers', 127–38 (*see also*
teacher wellness)
teachers' bias causing, 90–93
teachers' perception of, 5
unconditional positive regard in
overcoming, 97–107, 98t–99t
unpredictability created by,
72–73
vicarious, 131–32
trauma-affected students
as finely tuned detectors of their
environments, 35–36
inequity in schools for, 34–39
(*see also* inequity in schools)
mindfulness for, 40
punitive discipline impact on,
36–38
restraint data related to, 37
restraint impact on, 36–38
seclusion data related to, 37
seclusion impact on, 36–38
trauma-indifferent response to, 37
trauma-inducing response to, 37

Trauma and Recovery, 53, 191
"Trauma by Numbers," 53
trauma detectives
  teachers not, 110–13
trauma exposure response
  basics of, 131–32
  warning signs of, 131–32
trauma ignored
  trauma informed *vs.,* 172–75
trauma-indifferent response
  to trauma-affected students, 37
trauma-inducing response
  to trauma-affected students, 37
trauma-informed
  defined, 4
trauma informed
  trauma ignored *vs.,* 172–75
trauma-informed approach. *see also*
    trauma-informed education
  described, 5
trauma-informed classrooms
  relationships in, 83–95
trauma-informed critical pedagogy,
    172–75
trauma-informed education. *see*
    also trauma-informed practices
  ACEs in, 47–53 (*see also* adverse
    childhood experiences (ACEs))
  for adults in schools, xxi
  anti-oppression, 13*t*
  antiracist, 13*t*
  asset-based, 13*t*, 45, 82
  defined, 3–20 (*see also* trau-
    ma-informed education–
    related definitions)
  described, xix–xx

equity at center of, 12
healing force *vs.* buzzword, xix–
  xx
human-centered, 14*t*, 45, 82
interaction with equity, 27–39
proactive approach to, 14*t*, 45
school-related changes needed
  in, 15–17
social justice–focused, 10, 14*t*
start where you are, 17–19
systems-oriented, 13*t*
as trial-and-error process, xix
universal approach to, 14*t*, 45
trauma-informed education–
    related definitions, 3–20
  action steps, 19–20
  narrow definitions, 4–5
  new definition, 9–10
  shifting equity to center in,
    10–12, 13*t*–14*t* (*see also* equi-
    ty-centered trauma-informed
    education)
  structural lens, 8–9
trauma-informed mindset
  as job requirement, 140
trauma-informed pedagogy, 172–75
  critical pedagogy as, 162–64
trauma-informed practices. *see also*
    trauma-informed education
  ACEs as evidence for need for,
    48
  critical pedagogies and, 173
  defined, 4–5
  equity at center of, 12
  proactive priorities for, 142–43
  universal approach to, 43–80

as responsive supports for all,
62–65
SEL, 60–62 (*see also* social-emotional learning (SEL))
trauma as lens, not label,
55–66
trauma as more than a number,
47–54 (*see also under* trauma-informed education)
to trauma-informed education,
14*t*, 45
universal design for learning
(UDL)
described, 55
equity-centered trauma-informed practices *vs.*, 55
flexibility of, 76
unpredictability
trauma creating, 72–73

value feedback
in professional growth,
145–46
Venet, A.S., 88–90, 97–111, 129,
132–35, 141–42, 144, 152
verbal intimidation/threats, 33
vicarious trauma
basics of, 131–32
signs of, 131–32
Vietnam War veterans
trauma impact on, 6
violence
curriculum, 32–33
police-related, 30
racial trauma–related, 33
sexual, 9

stress and danger within schools
related to, 28–29
voyeurism
cycle of, 174

Watson, D., 30
Watson, J.C., 32
We Got This, 41, 155
well-being
fostering in children, 70–71
wellness
action steps, 66
as community effort, 58–59
critical, 58–60 (*see also* critical
wellness)
"cutesy," 135–36
defined, 58
equity-centered trauma-informed practices focus on, 63
fostering, 58–60
school leaders accountability in,
145–46
structures in understanding,
58–59
teacher, 59, 127–38 (*see also*
teacher wellness)
We Want to Do More Than Survive,
59, 66
"What White Colleagues Need to
Understand," 145
Wheatley, M.J., 18
White, S.V., 168, 176
Winfrey, O., xix
Winninghoff, A., 53
women
in STEM careers, 86

About the Author

Alex Shevrin Venet is an educator, author, and professional development facilitator based in Vermont. She began her career teaching English at an alternative therapeutic school where she later served as a school leader. Currently, Alex teaches courses in the humanities and education at the Community College of Vermont, Antioch University New England, and Castleton University. She facilitates equity-centered trauma-informed workshops for educators at all levels, including presenting nationally at conferences and as an independent consultant for schools and districts. Alex co-organizes Edcamp Vermont and the Trauma Informed Educators Network Conference. Alex's writing has appeared in *Edutopia, Mindshift*, and *School Library Journal*. This is her first book. You can learn more about Alex and follow her work at: https://unconditionallearning.org.

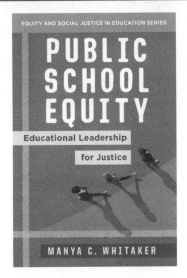
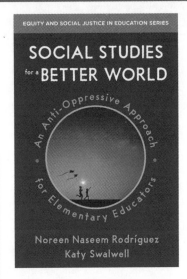
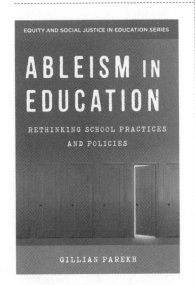